The Rose Café

Also by John Hanson Mitchell

The Rose Café

Love and War in Corsica

John Hanson Mitchell

COUNTERPOINT
BERKELEY

Library of Congress Cataloging-in-Publication Data

Mitchell, John Hanson.
The Rose Café : love and war in Corsica / John Hanson Mitchell.
p. cm.
Hardcover: ISBN-10: 1-59376-095-7, ISBN-13: 978-1-59376-095-3
Paperback: ISBN-10: 1-58243-445-X, ISBN-13: 978-1-58243-445-2
1. Mitchell, John Hanson. 2. Rose Café (L'Ile-Rousse, France) 3.
L'Ile-Rousse (France)—Social life and customs. 4. L'Ile-Rousse
(France)—Description and travel. 5. Corsica (France)—Description and
travel. I. Title.

DC611.L675M57 2007
944'.966—dc22
[B]

2006030693

Cover design by David Bullen
Interior design by David Bullen
Printed in the United States of America

COUNTERPOINT
2117 Fourth Street
Suite D
Berkeley, CA 94710

www.counterpointpress.com

Distributed by Publishers Group West

10 9 8 7 6 5 4 3 2 1

For my parents *(who endured)*

Contents

"You are astonished that I don't feel willing to leave a country so miserable as ours; but I cannot help it. I am as much a production of this island as its green oats, and its rose-laurels; I must have my atmosphere impregnated with the perfume of the sea, and the exhalations of its mountains. I must have my torrents to cross, my rocks to climb, and my forests to explore; I want space — I want liberty."

> Alexandre Dumas
> *The Corsican Brothers*

"Whatever shall we do in that remote spot? Well, we shall write our memoirs. Work is the scythe of time."

> Napoleon Bonaparte

"*Là, tout n'est qu'ordre et beauté, luxe, calme, et volupté.*"

> Baudelaire

The Rose Café

Preface

The year I turned twenty I was living successfully disguised to myself as a student in Paris, not doing very much about anything to advance myself in life and not caring very much whether I did or did not. In early spring that year, suffering from the aftereffects of the interminable gray of the Parisian sky, I went down to Nice, where I had lived for a while the summer before. Here I fell in with an international group of sometime painters and students such as myself who were biding their time in the little warren of streets and squares in the old city, on the eastern side of the Baie des Anges.

One of my friends there was an aspiring writer named Armand, who was the child of a local White Russian family who had lived in Nice since the time of the Great War. Armand had a German girlfriend named Inge, and in early April, the three of us made a trip out to Corsica to have a look around.

I had been living in Europe for over a year by then, first in Spain and then in France, on the Riviera. Up in Paris, I was enrolled in an independent study program at the Sorbonne, and most of my friends were either French or part of a loosely associated international group involved in the same course. The fact is, however, we rarely went to class. Education took place in the cafés, in particular in a certain bar near the Saint-Placide Métro stop where we gathered each day to argue over literature, art, and politics as if we knew what we were talking about.

Like many young Americans in Paris in that era, I had in mind that I would somehow be miraculously transformed into a writer in Europe. My intention, such as it was, was to escape from my predictable life in the United States and leave everything I knew behind. In some ways the plan was a success. I didn't know a single American in Paris; most of the people I associated with did not speak any English, and I had effectively disappeared into the European student community. But my notebooks remained empty.

Then, in April, I went out to Corsica.

We took the ferry to Calvi, on the north coast, and then drifted eastward along the shore to the town of Ile Rousse, where we found a small auberge known as the Rose Café, set on a tiny, red-rock island halfway out a long causeway that led to a slightly larger island called Ile de la Pietra. The place had a decent restaurant with a terrace overlooking the harbor, and a few dusty bedchambers above the dining room. We took rooms and set out on foot to explore the hills of the interior.

The Rose Café was utterly unassuming, a two-story building with a red-tiled roof and two French dormers, a wide stone terrace, a pillared verandah, and an interior dining room with a cool bar in the back. Behind the main building there was a promontory that dropped down to a narrow cove, bounded on the north by a small, rocky island, which was surmounted by a seventeenth-century Genoese watchtower, one of many that were constructed along this section of the coast to keep the multiple invaders at bay. Set in a nook on the southern side of the cove, just behind the restaurant, there was a one-room stone cottage with two small windows.

Since there were people staying in the upper rooms while we were there, I was assigned to the cottage. It had a narrow bed, a rickety table and a candle, and not much else. But it was perched high above the cove, and all night I could hear the surge of the waters below, the dark cries of seabirds, and the ominous howl of the local winds streaming over the mountains and valleys of the interior.

I came to like the setting at the Rose Café and would sometimes forgo the daily expeditions of the ever-energetic Armand and his companion. Instead, I would simply spend the day lounging on the terrace of the café, talking to the local people and walking into town in the late afternoon to take a drink at one of the three or four cafés that surrounded the dusty town square, with its pillars of old plane trees.

True to form, Armand and Inge grew restless after a few days and decided to move on. I stayed. The pace suited me, I enjoyed the gossip of the people from the town, who came out to the café every day to stare at the harbor and spend the night playing cards. I liked them. They seemed to have no ambition other than to live from one day to the next and enjoy whatever small pleasures happened to present themselves. I liked the view across the harbor to the *maquis*, the wild impenetrable scrublands of the island, which were scented with a wealth of resinous arbutus, myrtle, rock rose, and clementine. I loved to watch the bright little fishing boats set out each day to fish the nearby banks. I loved the lizards that collected around the terrace lamps at night, and the dawn song of birds from the high ground across the cove from the cottage.

In the end, I fell into a strange, perhaps unhealthy, lethargy at the Rose Café. I would rise early and take a café crème and a fresh-buttered baguette on the terrace above the harbor. Later in the morning, I would slip down to a tiny pebble beach in the cove below my cottage for a morning swim, then a morning nap, then a midday meal of local fish, another nap, another swim, a walk to town for coffee in the square, an aperitif at the bar, dinner, and then a deep dreamless sleep, lulled by the susurration of the sea in the cove below. I would sometimes awake in the mornings there and have to figure out where exactly I was, who I was, and what I was doing in this place. I was in a state of suspended animation.

It was a good place. You could easily lose yourself there if you so desired, forget that you ever had a past, or a future for that matter, and simply fall into that idyllic condition the locals called the sweet do-nothing, *il dolce fa' niente*. For hours, for days, finally for weeks, I simply paced through the uneventful days: swimming and sleeping and staring across the harbor to the green slopes of the hills that rose up to the jagged, snow-covered peaks beyond.

In spite of the languorous nature of the environment, however, in spite of the bright weather and the slow and easygoing pace of the people, there seemed to be some latent story in that place: some powerful, perhaps tragic, history that was not spoken of by anyone but which seemed to manifest itself in the ironic contrast between the brooding, snow-capped mountains above the harbor and the light-filled, festive air of the coastal community. I don't think I had ever been in such a powerful setting before.

I could not say that I was entirely conscious of any of this at the time. I was merely living day to day there, with no plans and no ambition. All I know is that, suddenly, feverishly, I began to write. Night after night in my narrow stone cell, I began to fill the notebook that had remained empty for over a year.

One evening, after I had been there for two weeks, *le patron* drew me aside and poured me a small glass of a local marc and began to question me about my plans for the next few months. I explained that I had nothing definitive in mind as yet.

"You have not the papers for France?" he asked.

"Passport, I have."

"No I mean working papers, you have none?"

"No, I'm a student here, I have a student card only."

"Doesn't matter," he said. "You want a job? Spring is coming. It's going to be the busy season. You can cut fish for us, sweep up, do the dishes. I'll teach you some sauces. It's not real work in any case, so the fact that you have no papers . . ." He shrugged.

"We'll pay you a little something at the end of the season, plus room and board. Nobody out here cares," he said.

"Sounds interesting," I said. "But are you saying that it's not exactly legal?" (Possession of working papers was an important issue among the poverty-stricken group of international students with whom I traveled.)

He stared out into the black waters beyond the terrace and then looked back at me tiredly. "You understand, Corsica is not — how shall I say it — is not well-known for its allegiance to the laws of the continent."

He lifted his left shoulder, tilted his head, and smiled regretfully.

He was a sleepy, unambitious man from Paris who wore the black-rimmed glasses of a Left Bank intellectual and always needed a shave.

I didn't know much about Corsica at that point other than the usual clichés. Inasmuch as Corsica is known at all, it is known for its vendettas and its notorious underworld connections, and also as the birthplace of Napóleon. More to the point though, I didn't know anything about the Rose Café, or its environs, or the people who hung around the café. But it seemed to be a place where any migratory bird of passage, such as myself, any refugees from any of the world's miseries, either personal or political, could settle briefly to rest and feed and enjoy themselves before flying onward to nowhere. I decided to take the job. Why not? I was running out of money, and in that particular year the American draft board had been sending me ominous notices requiring me to register for military service — to fight in an escalating little conflict in Vietnam in which I had no particular interest and whose origin did not seem to me entirely logical. I was young and apolitical and had perfectly pleasant friends in Europe who described themselves as communists — "enemies of the people." Corsica seemed a fine place to wait things out.

I went back to my old haunts in Nice to pick up my things and ran into Inge. She had left Armand in some isolated mountain village after he had decided that they must — they absolutely must — hike Monte Cinto, the highest peak in Corsica, even though there were still heavy snows there.

We had dinner and went out dancing at one of the local nightclubs. Inge was about my age, nineteen or twenty, and she had black hair and wide blue eyes — and many older gentleman friends with smooth tans who wore silk cravats and houndstooth jackets. I was never sure what, exactly, she was doing in Nice since she never seemed to have any money of her own.

We ended up that night in a café where there was an old-fashioned band that played Eastern European music. There were some local White Russians there, as well as expatriate Hungarians with handlebar mustaches. The band played old waltzes and polkas, and then an older woman in an evening gown rose and sang "Dark Eyes" and a long and sad czardas, a lament for her homeland. Grown men took out their handkerchiefs and wept, and when the band played the Hungarian national anthem some of them stood up, hands on their hearts, longing for some mythic older order that had been replaced by the all-too-real disorder of the current state.

At one point, while Inge danced with a tall Hungarian with hair cut *en brosse*, I went outside alone and leaned over the rail above the bay. The night air was warm, and I could smell the Mediterranean and hear the pitch of the sea and the sad music from the café. I looked out at the black waters beyond the lights of the harbor and was suddenly very happy to have fixed a place for myself.

Two days later I took the night ferry back to Corsica and stood on the afterdeck watching the lights of France sink below the horizon.

I have been thinking to write about my sojourn in that singular place for nearly forty years now, and the story that has finally emerged is probably all the richer for having aged. It's certainly more realized than it would have been had I written it when I was twenty. The only drawback is that the world has moved on since then. Characters such as those that once frequented the Rose Café hardly exist anymore in Europe. Language, social mores, attitudes, seemingly eternal fixed customs and beliefs have all changed dramatically. So has the landscape of Corsica. Thanks mainly to a huge influx of tourists in recent years, there are more restaurants and hotels, although the clifflike high-rises that have destroyed the Riviera have yet to appear. And yet, despite these changes, the mountains and hills endure, the maquis continues to exhale its scented breath, and the dream of the place that was is well remembered.

chapter one The Libeccio

*B*efore dawn that day, one of the older fishermen from the village puttered out of the harbor in one of the brightly painted little fishing smacks known as a *pointu* and headed northeast toward the continent and the fish meadows west of Cap Corse. When he failed to return in late afternoon, the others went out looking for him. Just before sundown they found him. He was dead at the tiller, his boat still motoring along, describing a wide circle in the empty green sea.

Other than that sad event it had been a normal afternoon at the Rose Café. Nikita the dog raised his head once and, without lifting himself from the terrace, issued an obligatory bark at a passing horse-drawn wagon.

At two in the afternoon the cat, Figaro, rose from his shaded haven in the corner of the verandah and sauntered across the sun-blasted desert of the terrace to a cooler oasis.

Down in the cove, Vincenzo caught three fish.

At three, Micheline and Jean-Pierre emerged from their afternoon tryst to drink a coffee.

And by late afternoon Marie returned from her daily sunbath on the flat rocks beside the cove and began to prepare for her evening entrance into the dining room.

But this also happened to be a Sunday, and by early evening everything had changed. Out in the harbor, the fishing boats were scudding home to port below the mountain wall; the ferry from Nice was just rounding the jetty; the sun was just skimming the jagged peaks that rose above the foothills; and down in the squally kitchen of the Rose Café, things were not going well.

Micheline was shouting at Jean-Pierre; Vincenzo was shifting saucepans at the stove; the waiter, Chrétien, was passing slowly from table to table still laying down settings; and Lucretia was leaning on the frame of the back door to the kitchen, smoking and shouting in dialect at her husband, Vincenzo. Within a few hours the weekly ferry would be leaving for the night crossing to France, and departing tourists and sojourners were already streaming down the quay. The residents of the upstairs rooms of the Rose Café, already familiar with the Sunday night push, were selecting the best tables for themselves and calling for service from Chrétien even before the outbound passengers began to arrive.

A Dutch family burst in, much burned by the sun and happy. Three Italian men in striped sailor jerseys seized a table for two, and then with the arrival of two women in their party, with much flourish and debate and squabble, began removing chairs from other tables and calling for service.

A party of French, probably Parisian, moved cautiously up onto the terrace, reviewed the scene, decided the place was not to their liking, and retreated. A worried English couple in sensible shoes came nodding politely forward. Swiss. A party of Germans. A swarthy couple whose language I didn't know, and on and on, as the crush on the single road out to the quay at the head of the jetty filled with traffic and handcarts and barking dogs and little troupes of families with children prancing ahead, and all the happy holidaymakers, homebound now for all parts of Europe.

Once the diners were seated and launched into their entrées, a young woman with a pixie haircut and hazel eyes appeared at the door to the interior dining room where the bar was located. She poised briefly in the doorframe, backlit by the lights on the terrace, glanced around the room to see who was there and who was watching, and then, with a light balletic stride, she approached the bar.

She had dark hair and full lips and was dressed that evening in tight blue capris, a white blouse with a plunging neckline, and silver hoop earrings. Just above her cleavage she had suspended a tiny silver crucifix. It hung there like a talisman, as if to warn off ill-intentioned suitors.

Chrétien rushed to the bar as she settled and, before she even asked, prepared a *citron pressé* in a tall glass with a china saucer and placed it in front of her, waving his hand with a flourish. This was, after all, Marie, the current love of his life, the reigning belle of the Rose Café.

"It was hot today on the rocks, no?" Chrétien asked.

"Too hot," Marie said. "I came in early for my bath."

"Oh, but I am so sorry," Chrétien said. "Naughty sun."

Marie had arrived with her parents a few weeks earlier and although she had many admirers, she had selected Chrétien as her consort. At the time, he happened to be the only one around the café who was about her age. He was a lanky young man with crinkly black hair and long-lashed, somewhat effeminate blue eyes who was a distant cousin of the *patron*, Jean-Pierre.

Just before the dinner push, I walked down the narrow path to my room behind the restaurant to get a clean shirt. I saw the German guest they called Herr Komandante standing on a promontory above the cottage where I lived, his arms folded over his chest and one leg cocked forward. He was a portly man, dressed now in a blue-striped bathrobe and white espadrilles. His thinning, sandy-colored hair was wet and slicked back from his high, smooth forehead.

"Been for a swim?" I called.

"Yes. And now I shall prepare for my dinner," he said.

"Jean-Pierre has done a good rabbit fricassée," I told him.

He considered this silently, nodding. One of his pastimes here was eating.

"And what fish?" he demanded.

"The usual," I said. "But Vincenzo has just come in with a big grouper."

"Good," said Herr Komandante. "I will take that grouper. Grilled. And I shall begin with a plate of urchins, or perhaps the fish soup, and also a green salad," he added. "You will tell Micheline, please. I will have one salad. Chestnut flan for the dessert."

"I will tell her," I said.

"And coffee."

"Yes, of course."

"And I will take my digestif on the terrace this night," he said as an afterthought.

People at the Rose Café used to mock Herr Komandante behind his back. It was said, among other unfounded rumors, that along with his love for food and sun he had an eye for young boys. But I suddenly felt a wave of compassion for him, here alone on a French island, a German in the midst of a people with long memories, isolated by language and culture, and seeking only to enjoy a few sensual pleasures. Who could blame him?

Back in the kitchen, the evening meal was in full swing. Chrétien and Micheline were rushing in and out, shouting for plates. Jean-Pierre was sweating and smoking, the ash salting his standard dish of grilled *rascasse*, a spiny red fish that he would season with myrtle, bay, rosemary, and other herbs brought in from the countryside. Micheline had started to spout her Sunday litany of complaints about the idiosyncrasies of certain diners; Vincenzo shifted his pans at the stove like a timpanist; and his wife, Lucretia, who helped on busy weekends, wandered in and out, talking loudly in patois and contributing little more than gossip about the diners.

I filled a copper tub with boiling water from the stove and prepared for the evening onslaught, and soon the dishes were coming in, one load after another like wounded soldiers from the front: first a table setting of soup bowls, then a few smaller plates, then some dinner plates, and forever, like foot soldiers, the silverware.

There was a perennial shortage of settings at the restaurant; it was not the cooking of Jean-Pierre and Vincenzo that slowed the service, it was the lack of plates and silverware. I had to wash, dry, and return settings as soon as they came in or there would be nothing for the guests to eat from. It was not so bad on ordinary nights, but sometimes on weekends, in the rush, the flood of plates and the swirl of dirty water and the outcry from Chrétien and Micheline for more plates came on relentlessly. No one was proud at the Rose Café. When a backlog built up and the main courses were served, Jean-Pierre himself would wander back and wash a few of his pots; so would Vincenzo.

In due time, as the departure hour for the ferry grew nearer, the incoming stream dwindled, as it always did. Chrétien sat in the corner for a few minutes, drinking a coffee and gossiping about the diners, his long legs stretched halfway across the narrow kitchen. Micheline brushed back her hair and goosed Jean-Pierre as she slipped by him with a tray of desserts, and then Vincenzo loomed behind me in the scullery door with a small glass of marc, which he set on the stone sink.

"Drink up, old man. It's over for the day," he said.

Now, in the quiet darkness of the terrace, the geckos emerged and waited in the little pools of lamplight on the white stucco walls, snapping at insects. The few lingering guests sat with their chairs pushed back, enjoying a coffee or a glass of marc and the night air coming in off the harbor. Herr Komandante stepped out from the warm interior of the dining room and stood at the edge of the terrace, gazing outward at the black wall of the mountains beyond the harbor, his hands jammed into the side pockets of his blazer. A fishing boat came in, its lights fragile against the vast darkness of the water, and slowly, one by one, the guests disappeared, and we were alone with the sharp perfume of salt air and the high black screen of the night.

It was at these times, just as the quiet little village on the other side of the harbor was putting itself to bed and the lights began winking out in the bedrooms, that the life of the Rose Café would begin to stir. Now the night crowd began to collect.

Max was the first to come in. He mounted the steps to the terrace slowly, favoring his right leg — an old war wound, they said. He extended his hand to me, limply.

"It goes?" he asked.

He was an amiable sort who always asked after my well-being and spoke English, although he tended to translate literally and had such a thick accent it was necessary to know French to understand him. Max had a pencil-thin mustache and always dressed in loose gabardine slacks and sandals with socks and a white shirt, open at the neck. He was from Ajaccio and, like many on the island, claimed to be a descendant of Corsica's most famous son, Napoléon. The rumor around the café was that Max had played an important role in one of the local resistance networks in the south and had been in charge of surreptitious arms shipments from North Africa. But maybe that was just another story.

Max walked over and shook Vincenzo's hand and then sat down heavily at a table at the edge of the terrace and stared out at the harbor.

Two more figures materialized at the far end of the causeway, walking slowly, one with a coat draped over his shoulders. This was André, who was accompanied that evening by a man with a long, sad face named François, who sometimes joined the nightly card game. The two of them shook hands all around and took their places.

André slapped a deck of cards on the table.

They stared out at the harbor.

André was fair, with blond hair and blue eyes and a slow, somewhat studied gait. In the hot light of the day he always wore sun-faded blue shorts and a sailor jersey. He was soft-spoken and smoked lazily, and would often sit at the edge of the verandah in the shade, nursing a coffee, his eyes ranging among the guests in search of newly arrived pretty women. I had heard that when he was young, at the insistence of his grandmothers, he had studied to be a priest and had worn short wool pants and little schoolboy caps. But he left the church altogether as soon as his grandmothers died.

The night drew closer; something splashed in the darkness of the outer bay, and then we heard the whine of an engine on the road to the town. A speeding motorbike darted out onto the causeway and streaked toward the café, its headlight bouncing on the rough road. It pulled up abruptly, and a small man with high cheekbones and narrow blue eyes bounded up the stairs to the terrace. This was the sometime glassmaker, Jacquis. He was a wiry type with extravagant gestures and fiery delivery, and whenever he won at cards, which was often (I suspect the others let him win), he would slap the table and shout victoriously, even if it was two in the morning and the guests were sound asleep overhead. Jacquis had many stories of criminal families who had devised ingenious revenges, cruel police, and hideous atrocities committed by the Nazis against the *maquisards*, the local resistance fighters.

Jean-Pierre ambled out from the interior of the kitchen. He had removed his stained apron and toque, and he wore faded blue trousers, a short-sleeved shirt, and worn-down espadrilles that slapped on the terrace when he walked. He took his place at the table.

"OK?" he said. "Shall we begin?"

André passed the deck to Jacquis, who snatched it up and dealt with practiced speed. The players fanned out their cards, eyeing them through their cigarette smoke.

Every night this same troupe would come out to the restaurant to play a card game known as *brisca*, a local variation of the Italian game *briscola*, which is played with a forty-card deck with suits marked with coins, cups, batons, or swords. Sometimes the troupe came out early, just before dinner, and would wander back into the kitchen sampling Jean-Pierre's sauces with hunks of fresh bread, brought in that morning by Pierrot, the little walleyed bread man. Sometimes they arrived with obscure women from the hill towns, and from time to time one of them would show up with a new consort from the continent. With the women present, they would play the courtier, holding out the chairs, bowing and scraping, making introductions proudly, and fetching glasses of cold rosé from the bar. On some weekend nights a band would appear, and the regulars would dance on the terrace, holding their partners cheek to cheek and bending forward in the *apache* two-step dance style that used to be popular with Parisian lowlifes in the old days.

But the constant there was the card game. It was a nightly ceremony that held their world together. Elsewhere, in the interior of the island in those times, there were still vendettas. Elsewhere there were smugglers and crooked politicians who conveniently disregarded the shipment of illegal goods from the continent. And somewhere out there in the real world beyond the red-rock shores and the green, flat seas, there were strikes and demonstrations, street bombings, wars, and revolutions. And always and everywhere, there was the aftermath of the big war, the war that shook the foundations of Europe.

Down in the dusty town square, every day at three in the afternoon, you could see old members of the Corsican underground with their long-distance eyes. They would gather there to roll *boules* and smoke and sit in the cafés and attempt to either recapitulate or obliterate their pasts. Sometimes at the local concerts, when the band played the old sentimental melodies from the time before the deluge, you might see a tear well up in the corners of the eyes of the older men. But out here at the Rose Café, on the little islet known as les Roches Rouges, the framework that sustained the universe was a deck of cards bearing the iconic images: the coin, the cup, the baton, and the sword.

Twenty minutes into the second round of cards, we heard a scraping at the steps to the terrace, and a figure in a white suit emerged out of the moist, warm night. Slowly, with a studied grace, a tall man climbed the steps and stood for a moment in the little stage of light at the edge of the terrace, his hand resting on the rail. He was dressed in a Belgian linen suit and a light blue shirt with a purple tie, and he had a deeply tanned face and silvery hair that he combed back over his ears like wings. Even in the half-light I could see the bright glitter of intense blue eyes.

Spotting the table of regulars, he walked toward them. Wordlessly, the players moved over to make space for him. Jean-Pierre spun over a chair from an adjacent table.

"Shall we begin again?" the tall man said.

This was the man they called "le Baron," a gentleman of uncertain origins with a slight Belgian accent, who lived in a large villa at the end of a cypress-lined drive on the edge of the maquis. Le Baron did not often descend to play cards with the regulars at the Rose Café, but whenever he did I noticed that a subdued formality would settle over the table. Jacquis did not win as often when he was there. The regulars did not let him.

From my first glimpse of this man earlier in the season in the town square, I had a sense that there was something different about him, some odd mix of authority and benevolence, or maybe malice that set him apart from everyone else in the town. I had seen his type from time to time in Nice and in some sections of Paris, but never here, never in Corsica. He seemed to me an emblem of an old, dying culture, some player in an elemental European drama that had once held the stage and whose retired actors were still wandering amid the ruins of the postwar continent. I watched as he fanned out his cards and glanced around the table. Every motion, even the slightest gesture, seemed to have an elegant grace, a phrasing of manners accumulated over the centuries.

Once I had finished the last of the pots I went out and joined Micheline and Chrétien, who were sitting apart from the players at a table near the verandah.

"They found the fisherman," Micheline said. "He was dead at the tiller. They brought him in at dusk. Apparent heart attack."

Micheline, who was probably in her midthirties, was originally from Paris. She had olive skin and a fall of curly chestnut hair, and she always wore striped Moroccan slacks and hooped gold earrings. People told me she had been a painter before she met Jean-Pierre, and I would sometimes see her sketching at a table on the terrace on idle afternoons. Once, when no one was around, I surreptitiously looked through her sketchbook. The images were all wild, heavily inked abstractions that bore absolutely no resemblance to the landscape that she would refer to as she worked. She might have found a name for herself in Paris, I suppose, but now she mostly concerned herself with account books and dealings with local deliverymen, carpenters, and plumbers.

The card game forged on, a slow, shifting drama of obscure events complete with incident and resolution, climax and denouement. The world was contained in cards: An explosion of matchlight against the black wall of night. The slap of a card on the table. The occasional exclamation of victory or loss.

I cleaned up a few glasses and went to bed.

Later that night, while I was asleep, the wind came up. I could hear it first ranging over the red-tiled rooftop of the little auberge with its emptied café and its papered upstairs rooms. The sound woke me, and I went to the east window and looked back at the harbor. In the light of the moon, I could see a strange white ketch with a wishbone rig just dropping anchor. Then I heard the surge of waves in the cove below my cottage, and then the wind took on a deeper growl. The libeccio was beginning to blow, the warm, moist wind that would swirl off North Africa, cross Gibraltar, and sweep over the Mediterranean to the east coast of Italy, hammering all the islands in its path.

The wind undid people, it was said. On such nights there were vendettas and dark assignations. On such nights, the Corsican zombies known as *mazzeri* awoke to roam the wildlands, wantonly tearing apart any wayward sheep or goat or dog they happened to encounter.

The wind unsettled me, too. On certain nights there, when it howled across the mountains and made ominous moans and whispers as it swirled through the rocks above my cottage, I would wake, light a candle, and write until it burned out.

chapter two The Nearest of the Distant Lands

In the old days there was a saying that if Corsica were a woman she would suffer great temptations, for she is very poor and very beautiful. They also used to say — still do in fact — that when you approach from the sea and the wind is right, you can smell the island before you actually see it. I don't know whether the first axiom is true. But I can attest to the second.

On my way back to the island from Nice, I went out onto the foredeck of the ferry and caught the scent of something — the sharp resinous smell of laurel rose and thyme, of arbutus, broom, and eglantine. It was the smell of maquis, the scrubby thickets of small trees and shrubs that characterize the vegetation of the foothills below the higher peaks.

Corsica was out there somewhere, still lost in the luminous emerald-green mist where the sea met the sky.

It was warm; the sea was calm; a spaceless green spread out before us, and astern the wake trailed off in two long white furrows. No wind. No gulls. And, except for the steady throb of the engines, no sound. It was as if at some point after the last of France sank beneath the horizon, we had become unhinged from time and had entered into an unbounded blue-green atmosphere where past and future ceased to exist.

Corsica is nestled in the northeast corner of the Mediterranean, a fist-shaped island of approximately 3,352 square miles, with a single forefinger — Cap Corse — pointed northward to the border with Italy and France. For three thousand years, the island served mainly as a stopover for the civilized world beyond, a harbor of refuge or at most a defensive outpost or staging area for raids on the mainland for the various cultures — Greek, Roman, Carthaginian, and Phoenician — that stopped off here en route to someplace else. The indigenous islanders were said to be savage and somber and not given to warm welcomes.

Odysseus landed on Corsica, Homer says, on his way back to Ithaca. He and his fleet put into a narrow island harbor surrounded by high cliffs and anchored there, hoping for welcome. Odysseus climbed to a rocky promontory and surveyed the land but could see no trace of cattle or any signs of habitation other than a few columns of smoke rising from the forested interior. He sent three scouts ashore to find out what manner of man lived in this desolate place. On shore, the scouts encountered a young woman drawing water from a well. The men asked who was the king of her people, and she pointed to a high-roofed house on a rise, the castle of her father, Antiphates, the king of this mountain-backed fastness. The sailors entered the house and beheld an enormous woman there, as large as a mountain peak, Homer says. She summoned her husband, Antiphates, who instantly snatched up one of Odysseus's men and prepared him for dinner. The other two barely managed to escape and fled to the ships, but the king raised an alarm and from all points, a huge race of giants, the dreaded Laestrygones, came swarming down to the harbor. They stood on the cliffs and rained down immense boulders on the fleet, sinking the ships and spearing the men who were left struggling in the waters like fish. These they retrieved and carried off for dinner.

The wily Odysseus had left his black ship at the outer edge of the harbor, and seeing the hopeless carnage, he cut the anchor cable. His men threw their weight into the oars and they sped out from under the overhanging cliffs and the rain of boulders to open water, leaving a wake as they raced away. The rest of Odysseus's fleet was destroyed, and, glad to have escaped death but grieving for their lost companions, the small company sailed on to the island of Aeaea, where the lovely-haired witch, Circe, resided.

Because of its isolation, its wild interior, its independent-minded, sometimes violent native people, Corsica became a haven for corsairs, contrabandists, and anyone else who preferred to live outside the law. In the late eighteenth century, after the publication of James Boswell's popular 1768 book *An Account of Corsica*, the island became a holiday stop for English gentry on the grand tour. Because of its uncultivated exoticism it was said to be the nearest of the distant lands. Trade and shipping of a milder sort continued into our time, and by the late 1950s, some of its more accessible ports, such as Ile Rousse, Calvi, and Ajaccio, became popular stopovers for yachtsmen from Italy and France. Nevertheless, even into the late twentieth century, the island still had a reputation as a harbor for underworld types and also a certain amount of maritime trade — some of it, as in earlier times, of questionable legality.

A minor incident during my first week at work gave me my first hint of all this. We were all sitting on the terrace late one evening after the dinners and the coffees had been served, when the local man they called Faccia di Luna — Moonface — appeared on the terrace, pale and sweating. He walked directly to the table of cardplayers and said something. Chairs were pushed back abruptly, Jean-Pierre went into the bar — moving quickly, I thought, for Jean-Pierre — and came back with a glass of brandy, which he placed before Moonface. They quit the game and made a circle of chairs around him, leaning toward him, asking questions, and then Jean-Pierre headed back for the bar. Micheline stopped him en route.

"What is it?" she asked.

"We don't know exactly, he is so shaken. Ambush or something. He and Lucas and the others were coming back from Calvi. At the turning near Lumio, two cars cut them off. Santini, he thinks. They leaned in the windows, waved pistols around, slashed the tires, and drove off. Just a warning, they said. Next time not so polite."

What was it all about, I wanted to know.

Micheline explained: Moonface was an innocent, slightly paunchy member of a large, perhaps shady family on that part of the island. He happened to have been with two more active members of his family clan coming home from a night in Calvi. A rival family, the Santini brothers, had — presumably — suffered some offense from the family of Moonface and the ambush was a little warning.

Historically, Corsica was famous for vendettas and powerful outlaw patriarchs who, though sought by various authorities from the continent — first the Genoese, and later the French — managed to lead successful lives outside the law and died peacefully in bed, confessing their murders to the local priest. In some sections of the island, the vendetta was the only governing principle until the early part of the twentieth century, and in fact worked well enough to maintain a functioning local agrarian economy, independent of the coastal communities, which were under the control of various continental nations over the centuries. Ruling authorities, such as the Genoese courts, would commonly favor the rich or landed gentry in their decisions, with the result that the local peasantry developed its own system of justice. *La vendetta corsa* became the stuff of legend and was often the driving conceit of Corsican literature (written by French authors, it should be noted). Prosper Mérimée's short novel, *Colomba*, had revenge killing at its heart. And Guy de Maupassant, Honoré de Balzac, and Alexandre Dumas also used the vendetta in their Corsican stories.

There was, unfortunately, a great deal of historical truth behind the legend. In one short thirty-year period in the late sixteenth and early seventeenth centuries, more than thirty thousand people were killed for revenge. The cycle of murder often began with an insignificant, minor event such as the theft of a pig or a hen, and then escalated over the generations as one male after another was knifed or shot in the back in payment for an earlier murder. The great eighteenth-century Corsican liberator Pasquale Paoli had managed to slow and almost halt the killings through the establishment of an effective and just local court system. But after the French government got back into power, the courts no longer seemed to be able to legislate what the islanders considered sufficient punishment, and the vendetta returned.

By the mid-twentieth century the practice of revenge killing had almost died out, and the last vendetta (or at least the last reported vendetta) occurred the year after I was there. There was still violence in the mountain villages, however — café brawls over women, underworld conflicts such as the little event that had just taken place on the Calvi road, and political differences. Two newly elected mayors had been shot at in the month before I arrived, for example.

Slowly, the excitement over Moonface began to wind down, eased by brandy and a bowl of fish soup. Moonface relaxed and became voluble. I could see him relating the story expansively again and again to anyone who stopped by the table who had not yet heard the adventures of the night. Eventually, he was persuaded to join the card game.

The next morning I saw a strange little freighter lying at anchor in the harbor. It was a known type, a single-stacked Mediterranean tramp steamer with a low, rusted, somewhat battered hull, a once-white superstructure, and a pilot house just forward of midships. It had arrived in the night like some otherworldly sea creature, and it lay grazing there at anchor, peaceful, unpeopled, and unexpected. From my vantage point, I squinted out into the sun, and was able to read the name: *Bagheera*.

As I was watching, I heard the spluttering pop of a motorbike engine, and Pierrot, the local bread deliveryman, arrived. Every morning Pierrot puttered out from the town on his motorbike with the bread for the restaurant. He had fashioned an oblong, insulated box on the back of his machine where he kept the hot baguettes for delivery, and as soon as I would hear his engine I would make some coffee and carry it out to the terrace. He and I would sit on the terrace every morning eating his fresh-baked bread with butter and confiture, watching the life of the harbor unfold below us.

He was a small, shy man of about thirty with one walleye,

and he dressed always in faded blue coveralls and espadrilles with no socks. He had been brought up in the maquis in one of those isolated stone villages where people raised sheep or goats, cut *bruyère* roots for briarwood pipes from time to time, slaughtered a pig or two in winter, and never asked very much of life. In fact, however, Micheline told me that Pierrot came from an old, landed Corsican family that had slowly declined over the last century, leaving behind only a proud name, a sizable tract of remote land in the hills, and a few feeble-minded shepherds. The last of the line, Micheline said, was the half-mad father of Pierrot, who lived alone with a herd of donkeys and imagined himself to be a squire.

I asked him about the new vessel in the harbor.

"Just *le Bagheera*," he said. "It comes. It goes out again."

"What does it carry?" I asked.

"Who knows?" he said.

All this was in April, and the heat was rising. There were days in that season that were preludes to summer, days that laid the dogs out flat in the town square and set the hens panting in the little gardens behind the houses on the back side of town. The mints and the rock roses, the wild carnations, a curry-scented plant called l'immortelle, and a flower whose French name translates as "claws of the mother-in-law" were blooming along the little path to my cottage. The heat waves shimmered on the causeway to the town, and Nikita and Figaro stretched out in the shade of the verandah, paws in the air.

There were always two quiet periods at the Rose Café, midmorning, when the visitors would disappear and there were no lunch guests, and midafternoon, before the real work of preparing the dinner began. Whenever I was free, I would take advantage of the time and hike out to the little islet beyond the café to swim, or alternatively, walk into town to take a drink at a shaded café. It was there, in the town one day, shortly after I arrived, that I first saw the man they called le Baron.

Every day the older men of the village would gather in the square for their requisite game of boules. They wore newsboy caps and frayed suits in spite of the heat and stood in small groups, with their hands clasped behind their backs, chatting and arguing and rocking on their heels. The square was dusty and shaded by old plane trees with pale leaves that shuddered in the slightest breeze. On the north side, there was a marble statue of General Paoli, and north of the square, between a few ancient, sand-colored buildings with red-tiled roofs, you could see the dazzling jade of the harbor and an occasional gull slipping by, white against a deep cerulean sky.

As was my custom, I had selected a table and was sitting with a glass of beer, watching the action in the square — such as it was. A dog, a brown, nondescript mongrel with bitten ears and a crooked tail, sauntered out across the plaza through the sun, nosed a fencepost, lifted his leg, passed on. At the west end, three mothers with baby carriages collected in the shade near an ice cream stand and a carousel. Down the alley where the pillared, temple-like market stalls were located, workers were clearing up the last of their goods, shouting and throwing cartons onto handcarts and stopping periodically to argue or gossip.

As I watched the scene, I saw a tall man with silvery hair dressed in a light-colored suit emerge from the promenade at the eastern end of the plaza. Like a stately white yacht he sailed through the crowd of short, darkly dressed men, greeting people as he tacked through, stopping occasionally to chat, often resting a slender hand on the shoulder of his cohort. He carried with him an oblong leather wallet and entered a bank at the westernmost end of the square, pausing briefly to check the contents of the wallet before he went in.

At the boule pitch, the old men collected in a line. Someone they called Henri, a short, balding fellow with a cigarette in the center of his mouth, prepared to throw toward the *cochonnet* (the little pig), the target. Henri squinted through the cigarette smoke, crouched, leaned forward, swung back his arm, and tossed. The ball arced across the sky with a backward spin and landed a foot away from the cochonnet — a bad throw.

"*Ai yo,*" the old men called.

Shortly after the game started, a little hunchbacked man came out of a barbershop on the north side of the square, locked the door, and crossed the open plaza, greeting people as he moved through the throng. He selected a table near me and ordered a pastis. The waiters knew him, and the old men called over to him as they played. House sparrows flew in and began pecking around his feet. He watched them, then fed them some crumbs.

"Everyone likes to eat," he called over to me.

"Evidently," I said.

"You are the American from the Rose Café, no?"

"I am," I said.

"I am Claude, a friend of Jean-Pierre and his people. Sometimes I go out there to play brisca with that regular crowd. You will see me sometimes, but not often. Those blokes there, they have the time. But I work over there all day." He lifted his head toward the barbershop. "I am tired at night."

"I saw you come out of the shop," I said.

"I work. As to the others . . ." He tilted his head and rolled his eyes.

We talked on for a while from table to table while he sipped his pastis, all the while keeping an eye on the game of boules. At one point, one of the old men retired from the game and joined the barber, and they chatted for a while in French and then switched to the Corsican dialect.

One of the reasons I liked living in Europe was that I was interested in languages. I was in the habit of eavesdropping on whatever conversations were going on in whatever language, even those I didn't understand. Corsican (which shares a lot with the old Genoese dialect) was difficult, but I had at least learned that it was a lot like Italian, save that all the o's were u's. When I was there, nearly eighty percent of the people still spoke Corsican, although almost everybody also spoke French, the official language of the island. Nevertheless, most would identify Corsican as their first language, even though they used French every day. Early on, I learned that if I wanted to ingratiate myself with the older local people, I could switch to my broken Italian, whereupon they would often answer in dialect and soon lose me.

I liked the interchange, though, and up in the little towns in the hills, I could often raise an amused appreciation among the old men lounging in the cafés by throwing in a few words in the local dialect.

When the two men at the table next to me switched to Corsican I listened all the more carefully, trying to pick out phrases. Then I realized that they were talking about me.

The older man broke off at one point and looked over.

"*Eh! Americane*," he winked, "*boum boum*." He made the sign of dropping bombs, fluttering his hands downward. "But never mind," he said, switching to French. "That's all over now."

He rose and went back to the game, patting my shoulder as he passed.

"He's from Bastia," the barber said. "During the war the city was occupied by the Germans. In the autumn of 1943, they pulled out. After the Germans left, everybody comes out on the streets and starts to dance and drink. Big celebration. Everybody happy — finally, eh? Then, while they're all out there dancing, the American bombers come in from Italy and let fly. *Boum*! They thought the Germans were still there, you see. It was a disaster."

He rose, said he must be going, and shook my hand.

Just as he was about to walk off, the tall man in the white suit rounded the corner and passed close by our table.

"*Eh, Barbiere*," he said in dialect as he passed. "How are you, old man?"

"Very well, sir," the barber said in French, "thank you very much. And you are well, I trust. And things go well at the villa?"

"Yes, yes, yes, all's well," said the tall man airily.

He had smooth, tanned skin and very blue eyes that seemed to have an internal light of their own, and when he spoke, he looked down kindly at the dark-haired, hunched figure he was addressing. "You'll let me know, will you?" he said, mysteriously.

"But of course, monsieur," said the barber.

We watched the tall man stride away across the square.

I couldn't help wondering, as we watched him leave, if he was one of the powerful local *capu* I had heard about, the notorious underworld figures, either French or Corsican, who control networks of smugglers and shady financiers, and maintain secluded havens in certain remote Corsican villages. This man seemed far too classy for such a role, as if the trifling concerns associated with money were below him. But for whatever reason, it was clear that he was accorded a great deal of respect from the locals.

"He's a good man," the barber said reflectively, as we watched him walk off. "He's from the north. A big family. Big château up there somewhere. Here, he has lived out beyond the town since the end of the war."

"What's his name?" I asked.

"Von Metz, I think, something like that. Van Zandt, maybe. But here he is known as le Baron. He's from one of those old noble families. Rich. Very rich, they say."

He touched my shoulder as he left.

"Take care of yourself out there at Jean-Pierre's," he said. "They're not the most upstanding group, those types."

I wasn't sure what he meant, but I let it go.

Out in the square, the old boules players had shifted in their ragged line. They watched intently as each took his turn. "Ai yo!" they shouted whenever there was a good throw or a wide miss. These were the old resistance fighters of Corsica's past. You could see the names of their friends and relatives inscribed on plaques here and in Calvi, and find little monuments posted around the island, announcing that here so-and-so had died, fighting the foreign invaders of this high-walled isle.

Everyone had assaulted Corsica at some point in its history, starting with the unknown race of Neolithic seafarers who set up the still-indecipherable stone menhirs and cromlechs more than 6,000 years ago in certain sections of the interior of the island.

Everyone wanted a piece of the place the ancient Greeks called
Kallisté: "The Isle of Beauty."

The best documented of these prehistoric invaders were the
Torréens, who showed up around Porto Vecchio in the south
around 1100 BC, ousted their predecessors, and began construct-
ing unique towers, or *torri*, which archeologists believe may have
served as crematoria in rituals involving human sacrifice. Then
the Greeks set up a trading post at Aléria on the eastern plain,
and by the end of the sixth century BC, the Romans moved in.

With the fall of Rome there followed a whole series of inva-
sions, beginning with the Goths and the Vandals, who merely
came ashore, destroyed cities, killed whomever they could catch,
and carried on. After them, the Saracens began making slave
raids on the coasts and even established a few coastal villages.
Finally, in the tenth century, the Pisans settled on the island,
established estates and fiefdoms, and began a rule of strict allegiance and tribute to the city-state of Pisa.

This evoked the usual reaction from the locals — a flight into
the hills and a determined resistance. The repressive Pisan rule
also had the effect of creating a system of independent Corsican
familial clans and local feudal lords, or signori, that endured well
into the twentieth century.

By the middle of the thirteenth century, the Genoese gained
control of the island. Once again, locals were evicted from their
lands, stiff taxes were imposed, and the great Genoese commercial trading machine began to subsume the island. The same
old xenophobic resentments began to smolder; the strict con-
trols only increased the struggle to be free, and by 1729, after
a minor tax resistance in the mountain village of Corte, there
arose a forty-year war of independence. The last years of this

continued struggle saw the rise of Corsica's most forward-thinking rebel, Pasquale Paoli. He was able to actually unify the independent-minded factions of the resistance, and he and his troops did manage to put the Genoese on the defensive. But in 1769, having spotted the Corsican-induced weakness of the Genoese, France moved in and eventually established itself as ruler of the island. Paoli's dream ended, and he died in exile in London in 1807.

Of all the various heroes of all the various resistance movements, Paoli is the best remembered, not only for his military prowess but for his attempt to establish, thirty years before American independence, a liberal constitutional government based on the right to life, liberty, and the pursuit of happiness.

The last invasion of Corsica, and the one most talked about, took place in 1940, when more than ninety thousand German and Italian troops attempted to take control. The presence of truckloads of Nazi soldiers patrolling the streets, the increased attention to curfews, increased scrutiny of personal documents, and certain liberties taken with virginal Catholic girls from Corsican families already known for inventive vendettas only served to encourage the resistance. As always, the rebels survived well enough with the traditional local support from the peasants, and the Axis forces met with such stiff resistance they found it necessary to install one soldier for every two residents, and that included all the women and children as well as males of fighting age. By 1943, the Italians surrendered. Berlin lost interest in the huge expenditure of forces needed to hold the resistance at bay, and in mid-September of '43, Marshal Kesselring began pulling out his troops and tanks.

Back at the Rose Café, there was a small, pretty Englishwoman with messy blond hair sitting by herself with a glass of beer. She had apparently wandered out to the island from the town and liked the look of the café and stopped for a drink. In spite of the fact that she was alone, she seemed content in her place, comfortable in her skin, as the French idiom phrases it. I noticed that a few of the male guests were looking over at her. The Rose Café was not the sort of place a woman alone would stop off for a drink. It was out of the way, isolated from the town square, and populated mostly with couples or the company of regular cardplayers who would collect there each evening.

Chrétien was in the interior dining room preparing the settings for the evening meal when I returned. He slowly passed from table to table, carefully placing each knife and fork and then staring at his work and making very minor adjustments, looking again at his handiwork from a distance, and only then moving on to the next table.

He was a graduate student in philosophy in Paris who had come down to work for the season and was a familiar here, having worked at the Rose Café the season before. He was fond of all things Spanish and used to spin off long quotes from García Lorca and sing traditional flamenco melodies after he had had too much red wine.

As soon as I came in he began to chatter on about his new girlfriend, Marie, who had been staying at the auberge earlier but had returned to Paris with her parents. She would be coming back soon, he said, deposited here during the week while her parents worked. The idea was that they would come down for long weekends.

"It will be a good season. She is very pretty, like a young

gazelle, but she is inhibited by the presence of her parents. With them gone . . ."

He held up a spoon and cocked an eyebrow.

He explained that Marie had failed the dreaded baccalaure-ate examination that is required for graduation from the French equivalent of high school, and her parents had settled her here in this isolated place, away from her many friends, to study for her second try.

"Their thought was that there would be no social distractions here," he said. "Nothing to do but study. A tutor will be coming periodically, but he has yet to arrive. Of course, I could help her, I passed the *bachot* with honors . . ."

He winked again.

Back in the kitchen that evening Jean-Pierre was preparing a ragout of wild boar, one of the island specialties. He had been marinating the chunks of boar meat in wine and vinegar laced with cloves, juniper, and mashed garlic, and he was now mix-ing together a sauce of onions, more garlic, carrots, and celery with what seemed to me a very generous helping of eau de vie. Periodically he would dip up a spoonful to taste the marinade. I noticed that his eyes would always assume a vague, unfocused look whenever he was tasting anything, and he would stand staring at the smoke-blackened wall behind the stove as if review-ing a beautiful landscape.

Island cuisine has four recurring staples: wild boar, seafood, chestnuts, and sheep's cheese, the best known configuration of which is a farmer's cheese called brocciu. Local wines, most of which were made from grapes grown on Cap Corse, just north-east of the Rose Café, were favored by the islanders, although less respected by French tourists except for a few rosés and a very good muscat, also from Cap Corse. Periodically, usually at some quiet midday meal when there was no one around, the staff would sit down to a long midday dinner and on these occasions Jean-Pierre would bring out an unlabeled bottle of a light-colored red made from a grape known as the sciaccarellu, which was local to Corsica and produced a wine that had, as so many local products did, a hint of the flowers of the maquis.

All these commodities had their seasons. Autumn was the best time to hunt and eat the truly wild boars. But in the interior of the island there were many feral pigs, and these the hunters would bring into the markets at any season. Like their conspecifics, the wild pigs would feed on roots and tubers and the aromatic vegetation of the maquis, which gave their flesh a unique flavor that was decidedly different from any farm-raised hog. In autumn, the people would round them up and slaughter them to make spicy pork sausages called *figatelli*, which were coveted by locals and visitors alike.

Jean-Pierre, who was the chef and owner of the Rose Café, had worked briefly as a journalist but had left France with Micheline for Mexico, where they attempted to live for a time with the mountain-dwelling Lacandon Indians. Things hadn't worked out as they had planned, so at the recommendation of a well-placed uncle, Jean-Pierre went to cooking school in Burgundy for a while. Before finishing his course he and Micheline gave up on this new career and came down to Corsica to raise goats and make cheese. That didn't work out either, and somehow they found the money to acquire the Rose Café.

As far as I could tell (I cannot say that I had a refined palate in those years) Jean-Pierre was a decent cook. But he had what I believe was either a local, or perhaps unique, custom of quickly braising almost everything in local olive oil and herbs of the maquis, finished with a splash of wine. The process would send up a fragrant thyme-scented cloud in the kitchen that would set my mouth watering autonomically, like a Pavlovian dog. Occasionally, he and Vincenzo would outdo themselves and prepare some elaborate local dishes — quail in a mint sauce, for example, or a boar haunch baked in Cap Corse muscat, or veal or boar with a sauce of bolete mushrooms.

The local types that frequented the Rose Café were not exactly there for the food, however atmosphere played an important role in Jean-Pierre's cuisine — that and the fact that the restaurant was at a remove from the village and served as a place apart, where any local could retreat and escape the tangle of gossip and intrigue of the village cafés and restaurants.

As Jean-Pierre was working, Vincenzo came in from the harbor carrying a couple of freshly caught fish, which he took back to my scullery and cleaned himself. Then he set to work on a squid stew he was preparing.

He and his wife Lucretia worked weekends, although I could not see that Lucretia helped very much other than to assist Micheline and Chrétien with malicious gossip. Vincenzo was dark-eyed, with a brush mustache and curly black hair, and his wife was an Italianate woman with a full-bosomed, nineteenth-century figure. The two of them spoke to each other in a mostly incomprehensible patois of Italian and Corsican and would sometimes get into shouting arguments at the busiest hours in the kitchen. None of us knew what they were fighting about, but in due time they would simmer down and by late evening they would all be out at the card game, Lucretia included.

Unlike Jean-Pierre, who seemed more or less indifferent to my presence, Vincenzo had taken me on as his charge, and when he had the time taught me sauces and the uses of certain wild herbs that Lucretia would bring in from the maquis, hugging them to her breast in great redolent bundles. She herself had the odor of wildness about her — you could smell bay and laurel rose in her hair whenever she brushed by you, and she too took a liking to me, and used to pinch my cheek affectionately and kiss my innocent forehead, spouting long phrases in dialect, presumably approving.

While we were preparing the evening meal, Herr Komandante poked his head in the back door of the kitchen.

"Tonight?" he asked in broken French. "What is?"

"A wild boar civet," Jean-Pierre said.

"Ah, perhaps," he said. "And what other?"

"*Rascasse grillée.*"

"Good. And as entrée?"

"*Soupe de pecheur,* if you like. Sea urchins. *Salade de crevettes,*" Jean-Pierre said.

"*Wie Sie wollen; alles ist gut,*" Chrétien said in passable German.

"Good. And then. What cheese?"

Jean-Pierre listed a few local cheeses, including the standard brocciu, a soft sheep or goat cheese seasoned with herbs that made its way into almost all the local dessert dishes.

"All right," the interrogator said. "It is good. All is good." He bowed, tipping his head to one side and nodding, and backed out.

This was a Friday, and a few new guests had come in from Calvi, where there was a daily ferry. There was a pale man from

Paris who wore tinted glasses and sat with an equally unhealthy woman, perhaps his wife, who had brought her own tisanes and her own bottles of water, which she had asked Micheline to boil for her. (After three days of this, Micheline or Chrétien would simply serve her local water from the kettle on the stove; she never seemed to notice.)

There was a stylish couple, also from Paris, who were clearly not happy with the isolation of the place, and also a quiet young couple from the north who were on their honeymoon and spent most of the time either in their bedroom or out in the isolated coves of the second islet where the Genoese watchtower was located.

Also in residence was a shy dentist named Eugène, with clean-shaven, chipmunk cheeks who had come out bearing a number of new suitcases and new summer clothes, apparently purchased for this particular vacation. He asked many questions about the region when he first arrived and seemed reluctant to venture off on his own.

The evening meal was quiet; only a few of the guests showed up for dinner, and washing the dishes was a simple matter. I was done shortly after the desserts were served, and toward the end of the meal Vincenzo brought in a tiny glass of marc and set it on the counter for me, a sort of communion ritual that indicated that the desserts were finished, coffees were served, and the real work of the evening was over.

I went out with it after my chores were done and sat on the terrace, watching the lights out in the bay.

The blond English woman I had seen earlier in the day was there, sitting with a tall man with an aquiline nose and reddish hair, swept back from his forehead. They were staring out at the harbor, not talking to each other. Herr Komandante was enjoying a cognac and a cigarette, smoking slowly and reflectively, holding his cigarette to his lips for a long time.

Chrétien and Micheline were sitting at one end of the terrace, seeking a breeze. I joined them there with my glass.

"So I guess you heard, Marie is coming in a few days," Micheline said casually to Chrétien after a few minutes.

"*Olé!*" he shouted, slapping his thigh. "Marvelous. Is she coming alone or will her parents be here?"

"Her parents will be here, but only for a couple of days, you'll be happy to hear."

"Oh my God but that is good. Don't you think?" Chrétien said. He turned to me. "You hear that? Belle Marie, the beautiful antelope. I cannot wait. You will be so pleased to meet her."

He blathered on, using animal metaphors to praise the beauties of said Marie.

"I don't know," Micheline said tiredly, "I think that you place too much confidence in her. I think you love her too much. She's going to fall for someone else as soon as her parents leave. Maybe that dentist from Lyon."

"Never!" Chrétien shouted. "She loves only me. I can tell."

Micheline lit a cigarette. "You know her?" she asked.

"What do you think?" he said. "She is too Catholic. She even attends Mass. She says she is a virgin."

Micheline snorted and blew out a dismissive cloud of smoke.

"And anyway," Chrétien said, catching Micheline's joke. "The dentist?" He began to laugh. "You cannot mean the dentist." The laughter consumed him, he slapped his thigh, repeating the word "dentist" over and over again.

Micheline merely looked over at him blankly.

A whisper of breeze rose up from the harbor and died of its own accord on the terrace. A gecko snapped up an insect from the stuccoed wall. Out in the harbor, the steady throb of a fishing boat engine fell silent.

I decided it was time for bed.

The moon was illuminating the mountains on the other side of the harbor and behind the town, just above the dark sweep of the foothills, I could see the three rounded, lower peaks that stood together in a line, like hooded, cowled figures. The locals termed them "the three nuns," and they looked down on the town as if in judgment of the world of human affairs. Above the nuns, touching the sky, rose the higher peaks of the interior. This was spring, and they were still snow-capped and glowing, white against the black sky. They hung there as if suspended above the earth, a realm of gods, who unlike the judgmental Christian nuns, were indifferent to the follies of the mortal fools below.

Around ten o'clock, on an otherwise quiet day when the heat was high enough to force anyone who was left around the place into a reclining position, I went to the kitchen and picked up an old fork, a mask and snorkel, and a fruit basket, and walked down the narrow path through the red rocks to the cove below my cottage, to collect sea urchins.

In the interior of the island, local game such as wild boar made up the signature dish of many of the restaurants, but on the coast, seafood was the specialty of the house. One of these delicacies was the sea urchin, which would appear on the tables of the coastal restaurants in spring, sometimes already cut in half for the guests, or served with a pair of scissor-like double-bladed pliers you could use to open the shells. Inside there were strips of red, salty meat that the locals would eat with bread and cold rosé or muscat.

The spiny, tennis ball–sized mollusks were found in large numbers in certain sections of the cove below my cottage, and one of my regular jobs at the café was to collect them. Jean-Pierre had supplied me with the mask and flippers and instructed me to swim out to the middle of the cove, dive down and pry the urchins from the rocks with the fork, carry them to the surface, and dump them in the floating fruit basket. The underwater expedition on that hot morning was when I first met Marie.

The tide was in that morning and the sea was calm — the green waves merely rose and fell serenely at the rock edges — and I could smell the sharp mix of rosemary, thyme, and sea salt that seemed to always collect at the narrow shore of the cove. I fitted the mask to my face and, pushing the basket ahead of me, swam out to the middle of the inlet, watching the seafloor.

Below the surface here, the water was crystal clear and the combination of light and distorted colors and shadowy forms created a dreamy, surreal environment. Vast, dark cliffs dropped from the surrounding shores into obscure chasms and crevices where bright-eyed moray eels lurked. Spreading out from these dark mountain scarps was a veritable sub-marine Serengeti, a long, rolling plain covered with waving sea grass, dappled with shimmering, refracted light and great, smoke-like shafts of filtered sun. Moving over this undersea veldt were herds of brightly colored fish, with flights of smaller fish above and, in the shaded valleys, the ominous, silvery forms of larger fish.

The spiny black urchins, with their toxic stings, were common in the cove. I could see a few below me, nestled in the sea grass, and I dove down and loosed them from their holds with the fork, and carefully lifted them to the surface and placed them in the floating fruit basket.

When I rose from the third dive with my handful of urchins I saw a young woman in a tiny bikini carefully weaving her way down through the rocks, tentatively, her eyes fixed on the treacherous path. She was small, with a mop of short hair, square shoulders, and very feminine, dancelike moves. As she descended through the rocks step by step, she balanced herself with a canvas bag, her free arm stretched out, palm turned upward. Curious, I sank behind the fruit basket and watched as she selected a sheltered, flat rock, laid out a towel, and then stripped off her top and lay back to sunbathe.

So as not to embarrass her by my presence, I made a noisy dive for more urchins, with a loud splashing kick just before I descended. When I came up with my handful of captured mollusks she was sitting up cross-legged and staring out at me, shading her eyes with her right hand.

"What are you doing out there?" she called.

"Sea urchins," I called back, holding a handful aloft. "I'm collecting them for dinner tonight."

"Good," she said, and lay back indifferently.

Once the basket was full I pushed it ashore and hauled it out on the stony little beach. The black mound of spines was gleaming in the late morning sun, and I stood there dumbly watching the reflected water drops on the moving spines as they waved slowly in the alien air. I did not feel at all sorry for these devils, having been spiked by one a few years earlier, one of the worst stings I had ever felt, worse than any hornet.

The girl on the rocks put on her top and came down to look at my catch.

"Why they don't sting you?" she asked.

"They're light under water, once you pry them off the rocks. You have to step on them, or brush hard against them to get stung."

"Are you Italian?" she asked. "You have an accent."

"No, American."

"*Oh là là, le cowboy*," she said, raising her eyebrows. "I like very much *le cowboy*."

"Not a cowboy. I'm from the East. No horses, no red Indians, no wild bears."

I said this because many of the people I had been meeting on the island presumed that there were still bears, cowboys, and

Indians in America. They also seemed to think I should know Marilyn Monroe and Joe DiMaggio.

The young woman introduced herself, holding out her hand, and explained that she was here with her "stupid" parents, but that they would be leaving soon, and she would stay through the month.

"Maybe longer," she said. "At least I hope longer."

Without prompting she began to tell me all about her life in Paris and her friends there, and a new café on the Champs Elysées called "le Drugstore" that served American ice cream sodas and hamburgers, and on and on about weekends with her parents at her grandmother's villa outside Paris and how her parents, or at least her mother, had money but worked as a journalist and spent all her time helping people like Algerians who really shouldn't be helped at all and in fact shouldn't be allowed to come to Paris in her opinion and how her father, who was also a journalist, had got himself into trouble for a story he had just published and how he had a mistress who, in her opinion, was more sensible than her own mother because she agreed about the Algerians and then, almost in midsentence, she asked if this was a good spot to swim.

"Yes, I swim here every morning. I live just up there. In the stone cottage."

"Good," she said. She waded into the waters and struck out for the middle of the cove.

She had a smooth stroke and strong shoulders, and when she reached the middle of the cove she arched down into a dive, and like a gleaming porpoise, slipped beneath the waters and didn't come up for a long time. I was wondering whether I should worry when she burst up with a great splash.

"Be careful of the moray eels in the rocks," I called as I went up the path back to the restaurant.

Chrétien was in the kitchen when I came in with my basket of urchins.

"You were in the cove, yes? You must have seen Marie. She is beautiful, no?"

"Cute," I said.

"Like a little rabbit," he said.

I hadn't thought that Marie looked at all like a rabbit.

"More like a sprite . . ." I said, searching for the word in French.

"A what?" Chrétien asked.

"*Une fée?*" I ventured.

"*Mais non,*" he shouted. "Not a fairy. Not at all. A rabbit. A beautiful little squirrel."

Things were getting worse as far as Marie's appearance, I thought.

"In the night, she transforms herself; she wears a hint of the best Molinard, just a trace you know, and you can taste the salt on her skin, and her hands, like the small busy hands of a monkey, so *delicata, si tanta bella.* I kiss her."

He cupped his left palm in his right hand and lifted it to his lips.

"She is like the small antelope that scampers beneath the acacia of the African savannah."

"She has a good walk . . ." I said.

Chrétien, I had come to understand by then, was fond of animal metaphors.

Later that afternoon I saw a new couple out on the terrace, taking the sun and a glass of beer.

"You see them?" Chrétien said quietly. "Marie's parents. Simone and Teddy. I cannot wait until they leave."

Simone had blond hair cut in a pageboy and the same hazel eyes as Marie, and she wore a large, flower-patterned muumuu, which she had hoisted above her knees as she stretched herself out at the café table, her feet up on a chair, an empty beer glass perched in front of her. I noticed how tanned her legs were, and her finely shaped feet — toenails painted a bright red.

Her husband was a small man, well formed, blue-eyed, but he had a surprised, almost frightened look as if he were unsure of whatever it was that he was saying or doing. In fact, however, he was a troublemaker, having published, according to Chrétien, a scathing article in *Le Monde* attacking both de Gaulle's policies concerning Algerian independence and, with equal vehemence, the policies of the colonialists and the right-wing French generals. Both sides detested him, Chrétien said.

"Somebody blew up his car a month ago," Chrétien said.

That Sunday night, after the ferry had left for the mainland, the man they called le Baron came into the dining room. He arrived early, while the dinner guests were still at their desserts and coffee, and sat at the bar. Micheline was in the kitchen at the time, and I happened to be at the bar when he came in. He settled in the front at the polished-wood counter and turned to face outward, toward the terrace, ignoring me. I think he was watching for his card partners, who had not yet arrived.

I had seen the Baron off and on over the past few weeks. I saw him in the square a couple of times, once standing under one of the plane trees with another foreign-looking blond man in a gray suit and a pressed white shirt, and another time with a large group of obvious continental types at one of the cafés. He would usually come out to the Rose Café later in the night, sometimes quite late, as if perhaps he had been unable to sleep and decided to entertain himself by slumming. He was always well attired, but in contrast to his appearance, he would assume a jocular, play-along-with-the-boys style once he was settled into a game and had had a few drinks. I would always go to bed long before the game was over, so I never saw him leave, although late one night, I saw him standing alone up on the promontory above my cottage. It was one of those nights when the scirocco was up — the moist, hot wind that blows in off the Sahara — and people were restless. Le Baron was standing, leaning slightly forward into the wind, his hands in his jacket pockets, his white coattails and dark tie flapping behind him in the high wind.

The promontory was a favorite watch post for locals and visitors; the site offered a fine view to the western horizon, and people often came out to watch the sun go down. Before I started working at the Rose Café I used to go up there myself. Sometimes after the sun had set, a lilac curtain of dusk would draw across the eastern sky, and the whole Mediterranean would shade from green to violet and then take on a deep purple cast. Watching the changing colors, I could understand the origin of Homer's enigmatic phrase "the wine-dark sea."

The little outcropping was also a night watch. Periodically I would see an old woman, hooded in a kerchief and wearing the traditional long black skirts, standing there. She was a widow, I was told, who had lost her husband at sea many years before. Later in the season I would sometimes see, very late at night, the Polish-born guest called Maggs up there on one of her sleepless nights, wrapped in her terry-cloth robe, and during the early evenings Herr Komandante would often post himself there to watch the red sun sink below the green horizon.

Lounging at the bar, le Baron watched the terrace for a while and then in due time he turned to me.

"You're the new man here, aren't you?" he said in English.

I acknowledged that I was, and he turned and went back to watching the terrace.

"Have you seen Max?" he asked over his shoulder.

"No," I said. "He hasn't come out yet. No one has. I don't know where they are. It's a little early, maybe."

"Maybe," he said.

Then he turned and faced me.

"Give me a Cap Corse if you please." This was the brand name of a local aperitif called *averna*, made from chestnuts, a drink favored along this coast.

I served him, he thanked me, and then he turned again to watch the terrace. He spoke with a slight French accent and refined English inflections.

After a few minutes he turned around again and sipped his drink, swirling it first in the glass, watching the lemon slice circle.

"You're in the little cottage in the back, aren't you?" he asked indifferently. "Did you happen to see a white ketch with an odd rig come into the cove late the other night?"

I said I had seen such a ketch a few weeks earlier but not recently.

He nodded and contemplated his drink.

"And where are you from?" he asked.

"United States," I said.

"Yes, but where?"

I told him I was from Englewood, a suburb of New York City.

"Really?" he said, taking a sudden interest. "But that's surprising, I actually think I know some people from there. Are there cliffs there, above a river?" he asked.

There were, in fact. The Palisades, which ran along the west bank of the Hudson for miles.

He said that he thought he had known a couple from the town during the war. They had worked with a church group around the internment camps east of Perpignan.

"They helped out with a milk-distribution network," he said. "But at the same time they were trading in the black market. Later I heard they began escorting Jewish children over the Spanish border crossings. Working with *chasseurs*, you know, the local people who help refugees across borders."

I asked their names.

"Pierce, I think. Mary and her husband, don't remember his name. She was very pretty, I recall. She used to dress in rather appealing clothes and distract the guards so they wouldn't check people's documents so carefully. I liked her, but her husband, he was a bit of a prig. Holier than thou. That kind of chap, don't you know. I think the Gestapo caught up with them at one point but they managed to pay somebody off and got free. I happen to know that they were very good at getting forged exit visas for people, letters of transit, that sort of thing."

I had heard of this couple and had even seen them once or twice at a restaurant called the Rathskeller where my parents would sometimes eat. I remember my mother pointing them out and telling me some stories about them.

"Did this woman have gray hair that she would tie back in a bun?" I asked. This was an unusual hairstyle for the period.

"Yes, although she had black hair back then. Very attractive, with straight dark eyebrows and haunting blue eyes. But how did you know them?"

"I didn't. I would just see them around the town," I said.

In fact this couple was active in leftist causes in the town and was somehow associated with my father, who was also a political animal and later had been caught up in the McCarthy scandals, as had the Pierces.

All this made me wonder why le Baron knew them — of all people — so I asked.

"I don't know," he said. "I was around that area at the time. One accumulates people as one ages," he said. "People. Things. Sometimes wives. They used to talk about their home a lot. I think the man, whatever his name was, missed his home. He used to talk about those cliffs."

"I think they were in some kind of trouble in our town," I said. "They were accused of being communists."

"Really?" he said. "They were such a likable couple. So you are a student here in France, I take it?" he asked in a friendly manner, clearly indicating that we were to change the subject.

I told him I was, and he asked me why I had chosen to go to school in Europe rather than America.

"There are perfectly good colleges there, are there not?" he said.

When he spoke to you he looked directly at you, with a

fixed-from-under stare. It was a gaze that was clearly intended just for you, as if he had forgotten altogether that he was there to play cards with the locals and had come solely to talk to me in particular.

I tried to answer, but in fact I wasn't sure I had an answer.

He carried on, though, and began to ask me about student life both in Paris and back in the United States, and the more I told him the more he asked. He seemed to grow increasingly interested in my life, and even began to veer into personal matters. Did I have a girlfriend. What was I doing in the neighborhood in Nice where I had lived (not a particularly savory area, I gathered, although I'm not sure I knew that then) and on and on, and all the while I was growing more and more interested in his life but was unable to ask.

Other than his wings of silvery hair and tanned good looks, the most characteristic thing about le Baron was his eyes. They reminded me of the sea beyond the harbor: bright with sun, ultramarine, with an interior light that gleamed even in the half-light of the bar. Whenever he asked a question he lowered his head slightly and fixed your eye confidentially. It was a little solicitous, and slightly disconcerting.

"What time is it?" he asked suddenly.

"Sorry, don't know," I said. "I don't have a watch, actually. The only clock is in Jean-Pierre's bedroom."

"Odd, isn't it? I have a watch. After I came here I put it in a drawer. I don't use it. Who needs it, I suppose."

"When did you move here?" I asked, turning the tables.

Before he could answer (if indeed he intended to answer) I saw his eyes light up, and Micheline appeared.

"Monsieur le Baron," she said with mock grandeur. "And how is it with you?"

"Oh, you know," he said, smiling sheepishly now. "The same, always the same. Living day to day. Dawn. Midday. Dusk. The year round. And you, Madame Green Eyes, how are you?"

"Busy busy," she said.

"Always busy. Give me another drink, please," he said to Micheline.

The weather had changed decidedly with le Baron, and the sexual repartee began to dart back and forth across the bar. I thought it time to retreat to my lowly scullery and the dessert dishes, and I said goodbye.

He lifted his glass to me as I departed.

Later, after the card game commenced, I joined Micheline while she sat smoking at a remove from the players. She would commonly sit in a lighted corner of the verandah after hours, reading novels and cutting the pages with a long kitchen knife.

"What about him?" I asked, lifting my head toward le Baron, who sat with his back to us, eyeing his deck through a drift of cigarette smoke.

"Oh him," she said, indifferently. "He's just another dog in the pack, although he believes himself to be from some old line of counts. He's from some industrial nouveau riche family up in Belgium. They made a huge lot of money selling coal, exploiting the miners and so on. They had a big villa and a title — so he says — but they probably purchased it from some defunct noble family. Then the Nazis came along. The story is that they took over his family compound as a command center and kicked them all out. They went down to Paris where they had a big apartment.

After that le Baron came south, to Nice, I think. But who knows?
Now he's just another crook."

"A crook?" I exclaimed. "Him? That classy old man?"

She shrugged. Blew out a cloud of smoke.

"Maybe not. I don't know. But he lost all his money in the war,
and now he's rich? Never works? Lives in Corsica. So what do
you think? He's generous, though. He privately funded a medical
clinic near here," she said. "He has also paid off the debts of a
few doltish peasants from the interior. He has even helped us
out from time to time."

"The barber told me he came out here during the war. He
didn't say why, though."

"He did come out here. Twice. But we don't ask why. Better
not to ask, sometimes."

I wanted to ask, of course. I never did like unanswered questions; they only served to sharpen my curiosity, and I never
had been able to leave things alone when told to. But so be it, I
thought, and went to bed.

There was a light cloud cover that night; you could just see the
silvery pale moon to the east, riding through the cloud breaks.
The high peaks were obscured, but the three nuns were throwing off a dull, sandy-colored light and seemed to have drawn
closer. You could see them hunched there above the town with
its little glittering lights winking along the harbor shore. Silent.
Ever present. Reproachful.

Somewhere up there in the hills, beyond the nuns, in the
twisted little valleys of the mountains, the old Corsican ghosts
must still have lingered. Here roamed the restless spirit of the
old liberator Sampiero Corso, who strangled his wife, believing
— wrongly — that she had betrayed him to his enemies. Here

was the bombastic self-proclaimed German nobleman, King Theodor, who, on the run from marriages, gambling debts, and political intrigues, came out to Corsica and led an uprising against the Genoese, declared himself king of the island, failed in that little venture, and died in debtors' prison. Here too was Gian Pietro Gaffori, who stormed the bastion at Corte in spite of the fact that the Genoese commander held Gaffori's kidnapped son over the fortress walls in an attempt to stop the charge. And perhaps, somewhere up there in the clouds, you could find the most restless spirit of all, the humanist and revolutionary Pasquale Paoli, who for the first time in its history came closest to liberating the island and, had he succeeded, would have set up a constitutional government two decades before the American colonists got the idea.

chapter four The Donkey King

News of the outside world did not regularly trouble this part of Corsica. But someone left a copy of *Le Figaro* at the bar one morning and I read it while waiting for Pierrot, the bread man. There was a front-page story with a banner headline. Algeria had finally been given independence.

This was big news. The Algerian struggle for independence, which had begun in 1954, had by 1960 effectively split France into several disparate factions. On one side were the pro-independence Algerians of the National Liberation Front, who had started the movement and were supported by the French left. On the other side were the so-called *pieds-noirs*, the European Algerians; and the *harkis*, the pro-French Arabs supported by the French right wing and the army. The French had sent in the military to root out the insurgent independence fighters shortly after the first uprising in November of 1954, but the struggle escalated into war, and by 1960 the reverberations reached France, with street bombings and demonstrations and even attempts on de Gaulle's life.

There were, of course, other events in the world at large in that year. Patrice Lumumba had been murdered in Africa — with the help of the CIA, according to my student friends. Kennedy had sent "advisors" (trained fighting forces, according to Chrétien and company) to Vietnam. Salazar had a repressive hold on the citizens of Portugal; Franco maintained an iron glove in Spain with Guardia Civil soldiers posted at rural crossroads throughout the country. Plastique bombs were going off regularly in the streets of Paris, and the OAS, the secret army organization, consisting of procolonialist generals, was still gunning for de Gaulle. Corsica sat in the middle of this maelstrom, at once indifferent and mired in its own problems.

We at the Rose Café seemed to provide a stopover and hideout for those in flight from these various political intrigues (myself included in some ways, I suppose). Uprooted African families sometimes alighted at the café restaurant. A Cuban refugee named Mendoza spent a couple of weeks there later in the season. A mysterious man named Dushko without an apparent country would often come out to the bar. And toward the end of the season, in September, a young French woman with mouse-brown hair arrived, in flight from Indochina, which the French had given up on in the mid-1950s. Russians and Eastern Europeans who had wandered out of the postwar camps for displaced persons that were scattered all across Europe occasionally stopped in, bearing with them their unfortunate histories; and southeast of us, below Bastia, the French government was providing agricultural lands for the pieds-noirs, some of whom would periodically spend a night or two with us in the upstairs bedrooms.

Corsica itself was slowly emerging out of the old traditions of weighted Catholicism, clans, vendettas, and insurgencies. In fact at this period, for the first time in two thousand years, there were no enemy invaders lurking off the coasts — other than French and Italian yachtsmen, who were generally tolerated since they brought in money.

I shared the news of the Algerian independence with Pierrot when he arrived with his bread delivery. He wondered about this momentous event for a while and then wondered aloud if that meant that more Arabs would be coming to the island. It turned out he was worried about losing his job.

Pierrot had invited me to accompany him into the maquis that day to visit his father, a man whom he talked about often over our bread and coffee. The two of them shared a flat on the back side of Ile Rousse, but in summer the old man spent most of his days up in the hills, on an old farm property that he owned.

Pierrot picked me up at the café later that day after his deliveries, and we puttered out the causeway from the café, motored around the plaza, and took a narrow street through the town that led back into the hills. As we passed little, faded wooden doorways, Pierrot shouted out the names of the people who lived there, including the names of a few of the regulars who would come each night to the Rose Café. Here was the house of André. Over there was where Jacquis lived, and around the corner was the place where Max was staying.

Beyond the town the road began to climb, and at one point below the hillside we passed a drive lined with cypress trees, with a sand-colored villa with a red-tiled roof at the end, set among landscaped gardens.

"Le Baron's place," Pierrot shouted back over his shoulder. "I have delivered bread there. A mute ogre guards the garden there. There is a woman in there, but she never leaves the garden."

The village gave way to cultivated fields, the fields to maquis, and the maquis to an upland forest of holm oak and beech. The road climbed higher, and we began to motor around terrifying bends over green chasms, some marked with crosses where people had failed to make the sharp curves. At some turns, half-wild pigs and cows loomed ahead of us and jerked out of the way at the last minute.

After a half-hour, Pierrot pulled up to a small collection of stone buildings where the narrow, paved road twisted up into a valley. From here, a stony, rutted track fit mainly for sheep and goats wound up to the left. We bounced over the rough terrain until the ruts grew too deep.

"Now we walk," Pierrot said.

It was hot in the sheltered valleys, the sort of greeny midday heat that undoes the local dogs. The high stridulation of the cicadas was filling the air, and we could hear the jangle of goat bells ringing from the surrounding hills and the clatter of loose stones in the gorges as sheep or mouflon, the native wild sheep, scattered. Deep, rocky brooks cascaded below us, stubby-winged buteos coursed above, and the air was thick with the tang of vegetation.

In time we came to a well-worn trail leading across some pastureland into the dense shrubbery. In the middle of the open ground I saw a small crumbling heap of stones, the ruins of a tower.

"*Torri,*" Pierrot said. "They are from the original people, a tribe who lived here two thousand years ago and practiced human sacrifice. My father says they are still living here in the gorges. He says they stole my older brother before I was born. Or sucked his blood. I don't remember which. He died before me."

We hiked on. Pierrot had a net bag of bread for his father slung over his shoulder that bounced rhythmically from side to side as he tripped along, and finally we broke out of the thickets and entered a pasture where a donkey was grazing. Around the clearing lay the ruins of old stone buildings, as if the area had once been a small town square or a large estate. At the south end there was a larger building without windowpanes, an open door gaping ominously. Looking out the door, as if he lived in the house, was another donkey. An old man emerged from behind the donkey and slapped its haunches to clear the way. He was dressed in traditional black corduroys and a wide-brimmed black hat, and had tucked his trousers into high calfskin boots. He had small, coal-black eyes and a crooked nose, canted off to one side as if it had been broken a few times. Pierrot kissed his stubbled cheeks and introduced me.

"Fabrizio Porto, my father," he said.

The old man smiled, revealing a piano keyboard of gold and yellowed teeth, pumped my hand heartily, and spit out a long sentence in a thick island dialect that I couldn't understand. He chased out the donkey and waved us in. I could smell wine on his breath, and garlic.

The interior was cool and squalid, the floor littered with straw and donkey droppings; it had a few bare shelves, a black stove with a pot on it, and a small wooden table with a red-checked oilcloth cover. Pierrot took down a big, dark flagon of red wine and three cheap glasses, and proceeded to argue with his father about the wine. The old man didn't want any, or didn't want Pierrot to have any, I couldn't tell which. But Monsieur Porto apparently liked me. He kept smiling and shook my hand again, repeating *Americano* proudly over and over. I think he liked the Americans.

After we had an introductory toast, we went out and sat at a rickety table in the shade. The wine was terrible, and I could feel one of those sleepy midday headaches coming on, but Pierrot's father was warming up: He addressed me in the familiar and talked nonstop, placing his hand on my arm and squeezing periodically, whenever he wanted to make a point.

"You must understand," he said, speaking now in French. "We are the last of the great Porto clan. My people, they married into the family of Napoléon. We had generals in the Grande Armée, skilled militarists who took the fields at Austerlitz and Marengo. We had big villas here and all through the south as well." He lifted his head toward the ruin across the former court-yard. "Now, nothing. Only the name. And Pierrot, here, he's the last of a great line."

He turned to Pierrot and spit out a torrent of dialect. I caught the word "girl."

"What's he say?" I asked.

"Nothing," Pierrot said. "Same as always."

"He should marry," the old man said to me in French. "He's the last. He should marry. And have ten children, all boys. And why not?" He winked at me and made an obscene gesture.

"I will Papé, someday I will, but give me time. I just have to find the right one," Pierrot said.

"He always says that," Fabrizio muttered. "Too much work, too little time, no girl around, at least not any good Catholic girls like he wants. All reading books now, and getting ideas. Better in the old days, eh? Womens is strange now. I can tell you that. Do you know how old is Pierrot?"

"No. Mid-twenties?"

"Thirty-one. No one is not married at thirty-one except priests and Nancy boys."

"I didn't know that," I said.

"Pierrot, he wanted be a priest but quit. And he's not a fairy. You're not a fairy, are you Pierrot?"

"No, Papé, I like girls — you know I like girls."

"See what I mean?" the old man said. "He's no fairy, so why not marry and have children?"

This brought the conversation down to individual families in the region and their available daughters, and then we began to gossip with him about the regulars at the Rose Café, all of whom seemed to be well-known to old Fabrizio, and all of whom had either wives, or steady mistresses, or many girlfriends. Fabrizio had lived in Ile Rousse, and he knew their fathers and mothers and all their cousins and aunties all the way back, and knew also the daughters of all the cousins and aunties, among whom, as he pointed out, were many marriageable women.

We finally got around to rich families in the region and then finally to the question of le Baron, who was, Fabrizio said, a newcomer to these parts but an important one.

"Why is he living out here in the countryside? Do you know? And how did he get so rich?" I asked.

"Le Baron?"

"Yes."

He waved his left hand and blew out a soundless whistle.

"He is very rich," he said.

"I know, but why did he settle out here?"

He avoided the questions for a while and then reluctantly explained.

"I will tell you. But it is not pleasant, so don't think about it too much. And anyway, that was all in the past. Now he shares his wealth. He has helped us from time to time, eh Pierrot? Isn't that so? He has helped us. He pays the tax on this land here. And we up here, we like to let bygones be bygones, if you take my meaning. He is good to the local people. Not a bad type."

But there was a dark side. According to the old man, the seemingly kind Baron had been a part of the Vichy government during the war. He and his informants, Fabrizio said, had identified all the Jewish families in the towns between Vence and Nice. Many of these families were rich, and these le Baron had befriended. He visited them often, sharing the stories of privation and the atrocities of the ruthless Milice, the local vigilante police.

"But then," Fabrizio said, "you know the story. There were commandments from Berlin. From Pig Hitler. They want the French to turn in their Jews. So Vichy and the Milice and the Nazis they set out to do the work; willing too, I tell you. In the meantime, le Baron, he makes his usual rounds of certain property-rich families in the towns just ahead of the Vichy operatives. He warns them — and it was true — that orders have come down from Germany and they are in danger of deportation. But he says he can arrange the necessary papers, letters of transport, exit visas. He tells them — and this was true too — that he knows people in Paris, that he has influence. He can obtain letters. Visas will surely follow, along with the permits, and even the tickets from Marseille to Morocco and on to Lisbon."

Fabrizio said that in the process of the various exchanges and forgeries and permits, le Baron also managed to legally acquire titles to the properties as a cover.

"Temporarily, eh?" Fabrizio said, scrunching up the side of his mouth and clucking. "We know what that means. Shortly thereafter, eh? The Milice show up. Families are marched to the town squares, and, whoosh, off they go into the trains and on to we don't know where."

He swept his hands together and pointed his thumb over his shoulder, toward the beech woods.

"Some Baron, eh?" he said. "But now . . ."

He lowered his head, looked me in the eye, held out his right hand, and rubbed his thumb and forefinger together. "Le Baron, *il a du fric*. He's got dough . . .

"Of course, we had our own problems up here back then," he continued. "But we're good hunters here in the country. A well-placed shot. One less Nazi. But we get by. We're used to that. The Italians, they see the way things are going and switch camps. They throw away their uniforms and dress like the locals. Even marry locally. You hear that, Pierrot? Even the little Italian fascist conscripts with no family name. They find womens."

Back in the town square, the old men were bowling. They formed a double line and watched as a middle-aged man in a serge suit stepped forward. He eyed the cochonnet at the end of the pitch. He crouched and swung back his arm, hooking the ball underhanded, stepped forward, and then, with a long swing, let fly.

The ball arched over the course, struck ground, and rolled toward the cochonnet.

"*Ai yo*," the spectators shouted. "Not bad. Not too bad . . ."

Another took his place, crouched, swung his arm back, and threw. The ball arched, landed, and knocked the first ball away.

More shouting.

Another player. Another round.

At my table in the square, the hunchbacked barber watched.

"Not so bad," he said. "Fiero is good. But just watch this one."

An old, one-armed man with his sleeve tucked into his left suit pocket came forward. He stood erect, *contrapposto*, the ball held in his hand and facing outward against his right hip, and eyed the situation. Silence descended. In the double line, the old warriors held their breath. Sparrows took flight. Glasses clinked behind me. A waiter stepped out from the bar.

Slowly the one-armed man held the ball forward, formally, as if in presentation to the gods. He drew back his arm, curling the ball with his hand facing his chest, and made his throw. The ball arched high over the pitch. It crossed in front of the shops at the north end of the square, it flew over the allée between the sand-colored buildings, black against the blue-green harbor beyond. It sailed onward, descended, and plunked down next to the cochonnet, knocking off the closest ball — the one Fiero had thrown — and then it rolled two inches forward to stop, nestled against its target.

"You see what I mean," the barber said.

And so it went. Winners and losers. War played with six balls and a little pig.

The English woman and her tall gentleman friend whom I had had seen at dinner earlier showed up the next day to ask for rooms. I happened to be the only one around the restaurant that afternoon, so there was no one else there to check them in. The English woman, who seemed to be the one in charge of things, said they had booked a room the night before and had reserved for a couple of weeks. I checked the book and found an indifferent, almost indecipherable, scrawl in Micheline's hand and finally analyzed the details. I showed them to their room and took their passports, which I studied after they left.

Her name was Magda and she had been born in Poland in 1926, which would have made her thirty-five years old. Her husband's name was Peter, and he had been born of English parents in Tunisia in 1925. The two of them lived now in London and were presumably married, although Magda did not have a ring, I noticed.

They stayed up in their room unpacking and within the hour, Peter appeared in his bathing trunks, carrying a net bag with flippers, as well as a mask and a mean-looking fish spear. He asked where he might do a little spearfishing. I told him about the cove behind my cottage, and he set off down the path. He reminded me of a gangly giraffe.

Magda came down to the bar a few minutes later and asked for a Campari and soda, which I mixed and set before her. She cupped her hand around the sweating glass, and then lifted it to her right cheek and closed her eyes.

"So cool, isn't it," she said. "It's been beastly coming over from Calvi. Steaming."

She was small and angular, with high Slavic cheekbones, blue eyes, and wavy blond hair, one strand of which often fell across her left eye and which she habitually flipped back in place. She had strangely elongated canine teeth that gave her an engaging, sad look whenever she smiled. Her husband was a sculptor, she told me, a former student of Henry Moore, and she was a professor of sociology at the London School of Economics. They had no real plans in Corsica, she said, but had come over from Menton because they thought it too crowded and had heard about this place while they were in Calvi, which they also thought too crowded.

"We are just looking for some place to lie low. And here . . ." she lifted her head toward the harbor. "It's quite beautiful really, with this view back to the little town and the hills and high peaks. And that island behind us, with the old crumbling tower. Lovely."

The Ile de la Pietra, the high island just beyond the restaurant, was the second gem on a necklace of the two islets suspended from the long causeway that ran out from the town. Except for a modern lighthouse and the ancient Genoese watchtower, this outer island was steep and unhoused, and cut with tiny green coves where cormorants floated. Near the tower there was a crumbling ruin, the site of the chapel of Sainte Agathe, which had been constructed at the site a thousand years ago. It was the presence of this red-granite island that gave the town Ile Rousse its name, Isula Rossa, the rose island. Beyond this outer island there were three other small islets, also unhoused. The whole complex of cliffs and islands, and the grand views to the west and back to the port, made the area into something of a sanctuary. It was a good place to be alone.

Magda, who I learned was known as Maggs, was a willing talker and was very good at initiating conversation about small, immediate things, such as the flight of the house martins that were beginning to build a nest in one corner of the verandah. Like many of the people I was meeting outside of Paris or Nice, she was interested in contemporary life in the United States, which at that time was out of the range of most Europeans and still existed as a mythic isle where cattle and bears lived side by side with a crass, commercial, empty-minded culture with no traditions and bad food. Maggs was intrigued by the current youth culture, which, unfortunately, I didn't know much about since I had been out of the country for over a year at that point. I had never even heard of the dance called the twist, which was all the rage at that time, for example. She told me that she had been a teenager during the war years, and had grown up in Warsaw, where, as she hinted, she had seen some repulsive atrocities at the hands of Nazi soldiers. I gathered from her descriptions of her life back then that she had come from a family that had some money. She herself had not suffered privations, she said. She merely lived side by side with adversity, which apparently was bad enough.

"I missed childhood," she said. "It was a very different way of life from the American youth."

The one aspect of America that she knew something about was jazz. Was there not a great deal of good jazz around New York, as she had heard, and what about the Negroes, were they really lazy and shiftless? And why did the Americans isolate them in ghettos and forbid them to appear in public, even though they had — in the European view at least — created one of the great artistic contributions to world music?

"I knew an American Negro," she said, "he was a great scholar and also a jazz saxophonist, and hardly lazy, he was a student at Oxford."

"He must have made a break," I said. "There are many exceptions, you just don't hear about them if you live in America. Even in my town in the north, the Negroes are isolated in a ghetto."

"As if they have a disease," she said dreamily, and spun the ice in her drink. She looked over to the town. "Like the Germans with the Jews; they saw Jews as a cancer."

"What did the Poles think?" I ventured.

"Yes, the Poles. Just as bad."

"Everybody's bad," I said. "Americans are bad. Bad to Negroes. Bad to the Japanese."

She laughed cynically, showed her winsome canines, and looked out on the town again.

"But what can you do?" I said.

"Right well I know what you can do," she said, flipping the hair from her eyes. "You can just forget."

She looked away. Her jaw tightened.

This was now the beginning of summer, and where I had come from all the colleges would be finished for the season, and the students of the East Coast schools would have dispersed to the resorts to work at the hotels, or teach tennis, or simply idle among the happy few that thronged the beaches of both coasts and all the lakes between, there to lounge and drink and socialize, while all the pretty little sailboats fluttered across the blue waters like flights of white butterflies, and laughter spilled out across dark mountain lakes from the porches of summery hotels. It was all sweetness and light, an ever-emerging present with no past haunting your every move and coming into the night bedrooms to sit on people's chests to keep them from breathing.

Sometimes there in the middle of the black, starlit nights at the Rose Café, I would hear some guest let out a terrible scream from one of the upstairs rooms, awakened by the all-too-real nightmare of the past war. Once I heard a vast, deep, male bellow, like a terrified beast suddenly caught in the jaws of a lion. Later I looked out the cabin door and saw Herr Komandante alone on the promontory, the night wind fluttering at the hem of his bathrobe.

Maggs swirled the ice in her glass and held it up against the light spilling in from the terrace and the harbor. A reddish glow from the Campari shadowed her face.

"Such a lovely sound," she said. "The sound of summer, isn't it? Ice on glass."

For dinner that night Jean-Pierre was in the process of creating a bouillabaisse, an *aziminu,* as it was called in Corsican. I was instructed to go down to the rocks at the edge of the harbor and collect virtually anything that moved — periwinkles, limpets, baby octopus if I could catch them, snails, crabs. These Jean-Pierre tossed into the stew pot along with moray eel, rascasse, *dorade,* and rouget; a coulis of tomatoes; plus healthy dashes of pastis and white wine. Vincenzo took on the perhaps futile task of teaching me to make a rouille at this time. He did this mainly by demonstration, lapsing into dialect or Italian as he worked, and even then giving only limited instruction:

"This! Eh?" He snatched a garlic clove and smashed it with the flat of his knife and mashed it around and threw it in a stone bowl.

"Then," he said, "potato." He scooped a potato from the soup and chopped it, flicking the knife so fast I could hardly see it. Then he took a pinch of a bouquet garni and threw it in the bowl, then chopped up a red pepper and dipped in a few spoonfuls of soup from Jean-Pierre's simmering bouillabaisse, and then began mashing the whole of it around with a pestle, all the while pouring in olive oil from an earthenware pitcher in dribbles.

"Now," he said, handing me the pestle. "You squish."

I took the pestle and began weakly mashing the mix around.

"*Mais non,*" he shouted. "Harder!"

"OK," I said.

"No, no, no. Mush it!" he said.

I tried again.

He took the pestle away and leaned into his work, pounding and swirling and mashing and dripping in olive oil until the whole of it took on the consistency of a thin, reddish mayonnaise.

Then he dipped up a teaspoonful, tasted it, and stared at something located far beyond the dark wall of the kitchen, something up in the maquis above the harbor, beyond the three nuns and the high peaks.

"More," he said to himself, and pinched in some red pepper powder and tasted it again.

"You," he said, handing me the spoon.

I could taste myrtle and thyme, rosemary, fish, potato, pepper, and a hint of salt and fish scale.

"Good," I ventured.

"Yes, good, now. Next time — you make."

The lesson was hardly completed when Lucretia appeared at the door.

"You!" she shouted at Vincenzo.

He turned to face her, cupped the fingers of his right hand upward and spread his left hand flat and lifted his arms.

"Wha . . . ?" he said.

There followed a machine-gun outburst in dialect from Lucretia that went on tirelessly. The tirade begat a counterattack that only served to increase the decibel level of the litany of whichever crimes he had committed that day (or more probably, the previous night). He pointed at her, shaking his finger, and shot out a short burst of flak, and then threw out his left hand, turned, and snatched up the fishing pole he kept in the back room by my washing sink and stormed out to the cove. She followed him to the back door and let fly another blast as he marched down the path.

"You don't know him," she said in French to the assembled kitchen staff. "Everyone, they think Vincenzo is a good man, a hard worker, pleasant to be around. Me, I know different. I know the other side."

Jean-Pierre shrugged and tasted his bouillabaisse.

Micheline retreated to the terrace.

Chrétien began selecting more silverware for the settings.

"What do you all know? Nothing." She turned toward me. "Only him. He understands me, I can tell. You know what a pig Vincenzo is because you work with him every night, is it not true?"

"I'm not sure . . ." I said.

"Oh, but you do, poor boy. Poor little lamb. Why, Jean-Pierre? Why do you sacrifice this poor American lamb to that animal? It is not fair."

She came over to me and threw her arms around me, tousled my hair, and drew me to her bosom, rocking me back and forth and looking back at Jean-Pierre over my shoulder.

"Look at him. He is quivering with fear."

"No, it's OK," I tried to say, but my head was buried in maquis-scented black cotton. She didn't hear.

"Poor lamb." She pinched my side. "You must give him more food, Jean-Pierre. He is too skinny."

"He's a student," Jean-Pierre said.

"A student. A poor, hardworking scholar, bending all day over books, never to see the light of the sun. And then at night, subjected to the cruelties of Vincenzo."

"He's actually nice to me," I muttered weakly.

She released me and stepped back, nodding.

"Just a trick. You'll see. I am a going to kill him. What else is there to do?"

She turned on her heel and walked out the back door. A second later she was back. She glared at us, snatched up a kitchen knife, and took the path down to the cove.

"What was that all about?" I asked Jean-Pierre.

He half-shrugged. "They'll be back," he said without looking up from his soup.

I peeled a few more potatoes and chopped some tomatoes and began cutting old bread for the rouille.

Ten minutes later Vincenzo and Lucretia came in together and set to work.

André came out early for the card game that evening and took a drink out on the terrace, selecting his table in the corner of the verandah so he could look over the guests from the continent. After dinner, Maggs and Peter appeared and took a drink at a table near the outer edge of the terrace. She was wearing a short, flowered skirt and a light blouse. I saw André look her up and down sleepily as she passed his table.

Peter selected a table at the edge of the terrace, facing the harbor, and they sat with their backs to the restaurant, staring out at the waters and not saying much to each other. After a while Peter got up, patted her shoulder, and went up to their room. Maggs stretched out her legs, shifted a chair over with her right foot, and set her heels on it, drawing up her skirt above her knees.

André observed all this. After a few minutes he got up, went through the kitchen and out the back door, and then returned by the stairway leading to the causeway on the other side of the terrace. He selected a table near Maggs, and stared indifferently out at the harbor, then called to Chrétien for a muscat, which he nursed silently. After some time, he shifted his chair a little, and said something to Maggs, as if noticing her for the first time. She answered. He said something else. She answered. And within a few minutes he had turned his chair toward her table and was carrying on like a tour guide. I could see him sweeping his arms back toward the town and the mountains beyond, and pointing out to sea. Like all islanders he spoke with his hands; you could almost follow his conversation without hearing it.

When I went back to my scullery, they were still chatting amiably.

chapter five The Professor

$\dagger$

Corsica has seven winds. In winter, the chilling mistral comes scything down the Rhône valley and the Massif central, lifting tiles from the roofs and screaming across the Gulf of Genoa to Corsica, where it is sometimes joined, or followed, by an easterly companion called the *tramontana*, which blasts in off the plains of the Po and is the bane of those living along the northwest coast. The scirocco charges up from the Sahara, carrying desert sands and hammering at Bastia as many as one hundred days a year. The *grecale* brings rain from the Apennines every winter. The *levante* storms in from the east, the *ponente* from the west. The *mezzogiorno* comes at midday and the *terrana* at dusk. And finally there is the libeccio, the sickle of the northwest coast. It crosses the Mediterranean and comes cutting in from the southwest, slamming itself against Cap Corse and beating the sea to a froth.

Very late one windy night, when the libeccio was blowing, after the dinner was served and the players had gathered for cards, we saw the local taxi come bouncing off the causeway. The car stopped and a small, older man, carrying a variety of black bags and satchels, climbed the steps and proceeded to the bar accompanied by Paul, the driver.

The new arrival was dressed in a neat gray suit with a white shirt, a tie, and shiny black shoes. He had a narrow, hatchet face and iron-gray hair neatly swept back.

"A new guest for you," Paul said to Micheline, with a decided wink.

At the bar, the new guest ordered a glass of cognac and announced that he intended to reserve a room.

"You intended?" Micheline asked.

"Yes, I meant to," he said.

"You intended, but you did not reserve?" she asked.

"The statement is true," he said. "Insofar as anything, in passing discourse, can be determined as truth."

"So you did not reserve a room but you would like a room. Is that what you are saying?"

"Yes, that would have been my intention," the old man said.

She looked over the book. This was mere ritual. She knew perfectly well there was a single room available.

"I am sorry, monsieur, but we have no rooms available," she said.

"How can that be?" he said. "I intended to make a reservation."

"But intention does not validate a reservation, monsieur, I am sorry."

"That is not, I'm afraid, entirely accurate, madame, if I may be so bold as to say so. Intention is, in point of fact, a reality. If you intend, it is so."

"I disagree," Micheline said. "One may intend, for example, to fly to the moon. But it is not possible to fly to the moon."

"Not yet," said the old man. "Perhaps someday we will be able to travel to the moon. If a voyage to the moon is intended, it will become a reality. Because it is intended, it will eventually be. If it is true that the room does not exist, then the discussion is not about the room, since the room does not exist. Conversely, if the discussion concerns the room in question then the room must exist."

Chrétien had been listening to all this with interest, and now joined in. He took the side of the old man.

"He's right, in a way," Chrétien said. "This is the puzzle of negative belief. How can you say that the room does not exist, when in fact we know it does. In other words, there is a room." He turned to the old man. "That's true, isn't it?"

"I'm not arguing about the existence of the room," Micheline said. "I'll grant you that it exists, it's just not available."

"Ah," said the newcomer. "The original proposition is true, then. Now, as to availability. The room exists, therefore I have a place to sleep, at least at some point in the so-called continuum of time. Now we must concern ourselves with the elusive question of linear instance. At what period in the normal flow of hours and days, say, would it be possible for me to occupy said room?"

"Wait a minute, just a minute please," Micheline said, abruptly.

Micheline was very fond of arguing. She could have carried on all night with this, but she was tired and merely looked again at the book.

I knew what was coming. She took out her pen and made some flourishes. Crossed something out.

"Let me see," she said, mumbling to herself. "If we move the dentist to the east room, then shift the honeymoon couple to the back . . . perhaps we could . . ."

"What does she say?" the old man asked Chrétien.

"I am saying that it's all right. I will make some arrangements. You will sign here, please, and give us your papers. The boy will show you to your room."

She aimed her head at me, as much to indicate that I was to play along as if to inform him that the auberge had a bellhop.

"Let me," Chrétien said, and snatched the old man's valise. They climbed the stairs and were gone for an hour.

"That's Marie's tutor," Chrétien said when he finally came down. "He wants to stay for a month."

A big yacht came into the harbor a few days after Marie's tutor arrived. We could see it tentatively nosing around for a good anchorage and it eventually settled just offshore from the café. It was an older design: a cutter rig with a single mast, a straight-stemmed bow, and a short bowsprit — altogether a fat, rather sturdy vessel. After dark we could see her lights and hear drunken singing and loud voices with German inflection echoing across the waters.

I was tired that night, and after cleaning up, I took a glass with Chrétien and Marie and then went down to my cottage to make notes and read. I was attempting to learn a little more about Corsican history at the time and was reading Prosper Mérimée's *Colomba*, the story of a reluctant avenger named Orso della Rebbia. Mérimée's female character, Orso's sister, Colomba, is one of the more powerful women in French literature: beautiful, intelligent, and cunning, she carries a stiletto under her mantle, and through her powers finally convinces her brother — who has been living in Paris and has evolved into an ineffectual dandy — to avenge his father, who had been murdered two years earlier by his ancestral enemies.

Mérimée seems to have had a penchant for strong female characters; probably his best-known creation is Carmen, the fiery gypsy who is the driving force in Bizet's opera, which was adapted from Mérimée's short novel of the same name. Colomba is equally powerful, although not as promiscuous, or as deceitful, as Carmen.

Mérimée lived in the first half of the nineteenth century and was a versatile man of letters and a member of the senate in the Second Empire. He was also a translator of Russian, something of an early cultural anthropologist, and an archaeologist. For years he was the official Inspector General of historical monuments in France, and it was one of his official tours of duty in association with this office that brought him to Corsica in 1840.

As was his custom, Mérimée immersed himself in the local culture. He traveled widely in remote districts, learned the dialect, and recorded the traditions of the mountain people. His fictional portrait of the Corsican culture, the characters and action of his novel *Colomba*, is considered to be a more accurate and controlled representation of the island than most of the other fictional or nonfiction accounts set in Corsica.

I read late into the night, and later I could hear the wind come up again. At one point I stepped out of the cottage to check the night sky. The clouds were slipping quickly across the half-moon and I noticed, standing on the promontory to the west, a lone figure, staring out to sea.

It was a man dressed in a pea jacket, the collar turned up high around his neck and his hands deep in his coat pockets. He stood motionless, almost like one of the upright stone menhirs of the interior. I watched him for a while wondering who he was and why he was up so late, a seemingly lonely, perhaps troubled person. I picked up the book again and tried to read, but I couldn't concentrate because of the lonely man. He was probably from the yacht that had anchored, and had come ashore to contemplate his demons.

Just as I was musing on his fate and the fate of all the lonely people who went up to this headland to think things through, I heard a gentle tapping at my door, and I called out to come in, figuring it was Chrétien with yet another night complaint about having been refused entry to Marie's bed. The door opened tentatively, and the man in the pea jacket loomed in the door frame.

"Excuse me," he said in somewhat halting, accented English, "I saw your light and this little hideaway, and I could not help wondering who lived here. Then I see you come out and look up at me."

He was about forty years old, probably German or Dutch, with prominent cheekbones and small eyes.

"Can one rent this room?" he asked.

"Maybe, but I work here," I said. "They've put me up in this place for the season."

"This is a beautiful house, high up, the great sea below. You are what, English man?"

"American."

"Ah yes, Anthony Perkins. I like the American movies. Have you seen *Some Like It Hot* with Tony Curtis and Jack Lemmon? It is very amusing, do you not think?"

Given the contemporary rumors about the sexual preferences of Anthony Perkins and the subject matter of the film my visitor happened to choose, my antennae went up, but I carried on politely and we began chatting about American movies, a subject that he was actually more familiar with than I was. As we spoke he slowly edged himself into the room, and, eventually, after ten minutes or so of talk, without invitation, he perched himself on the edge of the far end of the bed, leaning back against the wall. I was suspicious, but in fact there was no other place to sit, and we had a lot to talk about. I liked boats, and I was very interested in the cutter he had come in on and where he had been.

He said he was with a group of friends from Amsterdam, and they had chartered the cutter in Naples and were circumnavigating the Mediterranean. They had come up the Italian coast, stopping at various ports, and had then sailed over to Elba for a few days, then made their way to Bastia. Now they were cruising around the northeast coast of Corsica.

"That's great," I said. "I would love to do that sometime. I was on a little interisland steamer from Brindisi to Piraeus last February; we stopped at many little islands, some for no purpose at all. I vowed to myself I would come back someday and sail through the Greek Isles."

"Yes, the Isles of Greece. Sappho's Isle."

"What was that?" I asked, even though by now I suspected where this was going.

He laughed to himself, privately. "But of course, Sappho, you know about the poet Sappho, don't you?"

"I have heard of her," I said.

"She was a great poet, but you know where she lived, don't you?"

I did but pretended not to. I was trying to figure out by this time how to get him out.

"The island was called Lesbos. The women there, they loved each other, in that way, don't you know. Sappho, she was one of these. It is where the word lesbian comes from."

I grunted in disgust.

"But really, young man, you should follow your dream and go to the Isles of Greece."

He reached over and patted my ankle. I shifted my leg away quickly.

"You have a girlfriend?"

"Yes," I lied.

"Well good. That's that. You two must make a beautiful couple. I love the beauty of youth. It's why I so love Greece, if you know what I mean."

"I think I do. But for my part, you understand . . ."

"Yes, yes, of course I understand. And I now will be going. And so good night, young man."

He stood, paused at the door for a moment, and then fled into the night.

I had been propositioned before, but never in such a close setting, and as soon as he was gone, even though it was by now two in the morning, I went up to the restaurant to tell the troupe of my adventure.

They were still up, of course, sitting at a wide table inside because of the wind, slapping cards. They looked up in surprise when I burst in.

"What has happened?" Vincenzo said. "You're in shock."

I explained.

Much false consternation and alarm at the news. They threw down their cards and threw out their arms in horror.

"A fairy?" one of them shouted, "here in this very place? It is not possible."

"No no," said Jean-Pierre, shaking his finger vigorously. "Not here, not ever — why, this is an outrage! What are we to do? *Oh là là.*"

"We must hunt him down," André said.

"Yes, but what if he comes back while we're out hunting him?" Max said. "The poor boy, alone in his *cabine* — he will be molested and scarred for life. We shall post a night guard. Then go hunting."

"Just give him the gun," Micheline called over from her lighted corner, where she was reading.

"Yes, yes, get the gun," they all shouted. "An outrage. What horror."

They were braying with laughter and in fact didn't give a damn, but Jean-Pierre rose stiffly from the table, walked over to the cash register, and took a small revolver out of a drawer and checked the chamber.

"All right, then, you take this now. Go back to bed. If he comes again, just shoot through the door. Don't wait, don't ask, just shoot."

"Perfect," they said.

"The boy will be safe that way."

"You have to protect yourself at all times."

"You can't be too careful."

"Shoot first," Max repeated. "Don't ask."

I knew this was all operatic drama, but I played along and took the pistol back to the cottage, put it under the bed, and blew out the candle. Enough action for one night.

It took me a long time to get to sleep, and just after I drifted off I heard a gentle tapping at the door.

"*Jeannot*," someone said in lispy French, "*Jeannot? Tu es là. Est-ce que je peux entrer encore?*"

My erstwhile night visitor had spoken in English, so I knew it was someone from the troupe.

I thought of firing a few rounds out the window to scare him but instead shouted *"Fous le camp ou je tirerai,"* and kicked open the door.

There was Jean-Pierre, crouching against the wall, and two or three others up on the rocks, watching.

"What if I had believed you and shot through the door?" I asked.

Vincenzo, who had not been there, asked me all about this incident the next day while I was peeling potatoes. He too found it amusing, but he was less tolerant of the poor lonely man.

"No one cares what he does, but he should stick to his own kind," he said definitively.

"I suppose," I said. "He actually did leave me alone. I probably should never have let him in."

To change the subject I told him about my visit with Fabrizio.

"Ah yes," he said. "The old impostor."

"What do you mean?" I asked.

"He thinks he's from some great Corsican family, a cousin of Napoléon of course, but in fact he's just like anyone else. If that family ever had money it's because they stole it. Now they have nothing. Just a few donkeys and chickens."

I told him Fabrizio's story of le Baron.

"He told me le Baron made his money stealing Jewish properties around Nice during the war," I said.

This begat one of Vincenzo's great rolling outbursts of laughter. He had a laugh that would cause the diners to pause, midbite, whenever it spilled out of the kitchen.

"Fabrizio?" he shouted. "He said that? And you believed it?"

"Why?" I asked. "Shouldn't I have?"

"You didn't hear about old Fabrizio, did you? What they say ..."

I told him no, but he seemed a friendly old man.

"By day, yes," Vincenzo said. "By night, some people say he is one of the mazzeri." He started laughing again.

In certain sections in the interior of Corsica, you could still find the ancient menhirs constructed by megalithic cultures who lived on the island and practiced their chthonic faith well into the Christian era. I later learned that some of the traditions of these ancient death cults were still practiced on the island, including the curious tradition of the night walkers known as mazzeri. Even as late as the 1960s there were said to be a few mazzeri living in the mountain villages. As far as I could understand, they were a Corsican species of zombie, living dead, who seemed to be slightly eccentric individuals who went about their business during the day but by night transformed themselves into walking dead who circulated in the interior valleys, killing sheep and goats, and on some occasions, pet dogs or even people. They were unable to stop themselves, it was said.

Traditionally, in the interior hill towns of Corsica, people believed that the soul of someone who was going to die would desert the body one year to the day before the actual death. And from time to time, out on their night forays in the maquis, the mazzeri would come upon the funeral procession of someone who had not yet died. The mazzeri were therefore able to say — if asked in the proper stylistic manner — who was going to be dying in any given year. Not that it would do anyone any good to know. Once your fate had been sealed, there was no escape. I later heard stories of peasants trading their best sheep or cows to a mazzero to intervene in a foretold death, but it never did any good.

Vincenzo, who was from the interior but lived in the cosmopolitan town of Ile Rousse, knew a little of both worlds. He said that basically, the mazzeri, as far as he was concerned, were just the sort of people that turn up in any small village anywhere in the world. Eccentric types, who for whatever reason, separate themselves from the normal customs of daily life — including the church.

"Back in the mountains, they don't understand this. So they revert to this mazzeri legend," Vincenzo said. "That's what they say about old Fabrizio, just because he prefers to live up there in the ruins of his old property."

Vincenzo told me that there were also still a few *signadore* living up in the mountain villages. These were a form of white witch who were also able to predict the future and could break the spell of the evil eye, the *occhju*, through ritualistic practices. To predict the presence of evil, or things to come, they would spill a few drops of oil in a china dish filled with water and read events through the patterns of the floating oil drops. They were able to absorb this evil into themselves, whereupon they would grow mysteriously ill and then recover, having saved the soul of the petitioner. They were, Vincenzo said, especially powerful on Christmas night, when — as everyone knew — all the evil spirits would be forced into hiding.

"But all that . . ." Vincenzo said with a wave ". . . just myth. Nowadays, no one believes that nonsense but a few old crones. Maybe there is some crazy old signadora up there in that valley who started spreading rumors about Fabrizio, just because he's a little off center and collects donkeys. They are probably the same ones who say he was a collaborator. Which of course, is not true. If Fabrizio had helped the Nazis he wouldn't be alive today."

The fact is, Vincenzo said, Fabrizio had the habit of ingratiating himself with the invaders, either Italian or German, and then once he had their trust, murdering them. The old man had operated on his own and was not really a part of any organized network.

I thought this sounded like a reversal of Fabrizio's story on the background of le Baron. But Fabrizio had le Baron's history mixed up, according to Vincenzo. He said that le Baron was not associated with the Vichy regime, although he had indeed lived around Nice during the war. He worked in a bank but had acquired his real money by trafficking in the black market, arranging imports and then privately financing the underground. No one in the Vichy government suspected him because of the bank job and his formal demeanor, and the way he would appear at the casinos with Nazi officers and Vichy authorities. He would buy champagne for everyone, gamble freely, and talk loudly against the terrorists who blew up German supply trains.

"He was never one of the rough-dressed country types who camped up in the hills and blew up trucks," Vincenzo said. "Everybody knows that. He was a gentleman, always dressed well, but when things got hot around Nice, he came out here and disappeared into the maquis. That's when le Baron rumor started. But the Belgian accent is a fake. You listen carefully, you can hear. He's French. Alsatian maybe — somewhere up there in the north."

I asked him how he knew all this.

"Common knowledge. Go ask any old maquisard, like Max. They knew him back then. Although, I have to say, I think Fabrizio knew him too. He hid him the first time he was here."

I asked why no one else had told me all this.

"Anyone who?"

"Jean-Pierre, for example. Micheline …"

He laughed again. "Well, Micheline should know," he said.

He raised his eyebrows as if he knew something more than he was willing to tell.

"But what can the two of them really know about anything? They're foreigners. They're from Paris. No one from Paris knows anything. And anyway, what do they say about him?"

"Nothing."

"Well at least they're honest," he said.

I took over the bar later that evening, just before the dinner push began. Giancarlo the tutor was there, sitting with Herr Komandante and chatting fluently in German. I only caught a few words in their enthusiastic mutual interest. "*Ja*, Rilke. Ah, Rilke," Herr Komandante said, placing his hand on his heart and tilting his head to the sky. Then Giancarlo drilled in and deflated whatever enthusiasm had swept Herr Komandante away.

I noticed that in French Giancarlo had the hard *r*'s of the local accent, and after Herr Komandante went off to his table, just to make conversation I made the mistake of asking him where he was from.

"Where am I from?" Giancarlo asked rhetorically. He let out a long, dramatic sigh. "This is an admirable question, my son," he said. "In the current state of time and place as we perceive it, I am from Paris. That is to say I have traveled here to the Isle of Beauty from the city of Paris. I also happen to reside in that city. However, if you were to put the question to me in the larger context, that is to say, where was I before I was in Paris, or in what part of the European continent were my progenitors settled on the day in which I was born, and how came they to be in Europe at all, having emigrated, in all likelihood, up from the Indian subcontinent, or across the steppes of Asia, since we are all, as you know, migrants on this earth. If you were to phrase the question in this manner, then you would say I am, most recently, from Italy. From Verona."

I nodded and busied myself behind the bar. But he carried on.

"My people lived in or near Verona for a number of centuries and before that, in the time of the Republic, in Rome. In my time, which is to say in time of war, for reasons of a political nature, I wandered from my native place."

I made clear gestures to complete my work at the bar and move on, but he continued.

"You see," he said, leaning forward conspiratorially and lowering his voice, "I am a descendant on my mother's side from the tribe of Judea, and therefore, under the last regime, my family was considered suspect. This, to us, was a great awakening, since we were, as far as we knew, nothing more rare than Italians of an irreligious persuasion, having rejected virtually all the opiates of comforting myths. Another glass, if you please," he said, interrupting himself.

I brought over a bottle of local rosé and filled his glass.

"Now, with the rising waters of the deluge, and with the increasing pressure upon the Chosen People, I decided, in spite of my irreligiosity, to replay the role of the Wandering Jew. And so, to answer your question briefly, I have accepted teaching posts in various cities of the European continent. But during the last conflict, in that time in which the tribes of the dark forests of Germania emerged once again to launch an attack on civilization, I happen to have been in Paris. The grandparents of Marie, with whom I was acquainted through my work at the university, saw to my well-being, and their intervention and invention provided me with the necessary papers, proving to any suspect authorities of the occupying forces that I was a devoted member of the Church of Rome."

He reached into his coat pocket and drew out a rosary.

"My passport," he said. "I still carry it with me. Just in case."

chapter six Red Sails
in the Sunset

$\rightarrow$

In the late afternoon on a Friday, I came up to the kitchen from a nap to make some coffee and found Vincenzo already at work, preparing a new sauce espagnole, a base created from meat stock that had already been simmering for a few hours. He would use this off and on during the whole week in the preparation of other sauces.

"Halo," he called over his shoulder when I came in. "More fish. Big night tonight. Some gypsy musicians have come through, and Micheline has talked them into performing here in exchange for a good dinner."

He shifted the sauce pot, ducked down to check the flame, and then came over and showed me a heap of fish all jumbled together in the sink.

It had taken me a while to sort out all the different species of fish and other marine life that I had to deal with at the Rose Café. They would eat anything from the sea — eels and tiny snails, all manner of crustaceans including baby crabs, which they would consume whole, whelks and limpets and periwinkles, and all sizes of octopus and squid, and oysters and clams, urchins of course, and finfish ranging from glittering sardine-like things all the way up to groupers and huge tunas that Jean-Pierre himself would sometimes spear. All these I had to clean in one manner or another, and I dealt with such a huge variety that I never did learn the English names for many of the species I commonly had to scale and gut.

Jean-Pierre's standard cooking method was either to grill or bake these species, although Vincenzo had a specialty called *grondin aux olives*, an oven-baked gurnard, which he served with a spicy sauce that he would make with egg, olive oil, tomatoes, vinegar, and olives. He and Jean-Pierre also had a standard baked mullet made with an onion sauce spiced with fennel, a plant that grew right outside the back door of the kitchen. When they were short on freshly collected bunches, they would dash out the back door and grab a handful. The same was true for fresh fish. Vincenzo kept a fishing rod by the back door, and whenever he had a few minutes free in the kitchen, he would dash down to the rocks and make a cast into the cove. If he didn't catch anything, he would come back in through the kitchen door. But if he was successful, he would return by way of the terrace and the dining room, the fish still flopping on the hook.

One of the regular species that I had to clean was the red-scaled rascasse. Mistakenly termed scorpion fish in English, it is in fact a different species altogether and a standard ingredient of bouillabaisse, although it is also grilled and sometimes baked separately. The rascasse has a nasty ridge of toxic spines on its dorsal fins. I had been warned by Vincenzo when I first began cutting fish not to get pricked by them, but no matter how careful I was, at some point every time I cleaned fish, I would get stuck. My fingers would swell and ache for a day or so, and then, as soon as I recovered, I would get stung again.

That Friday afternoon I carried the mess of fish to the rocks at the harbor in a fruit basket and began scaling and gutting them,

tipping the offal into the clear waters. Within a minute I began
to see dark forms coming in to feed on the remains.

Just as I was finishing up and cleaning the knives, Marie joined
me, and we sat watching the underwater life crawl, dart, or float
out from the obscure crevices and depths to feed on the fish
innards.

As we watched the marine life, she leaned closer to me and
at one point hooked her arm over my knee to hold herself up.
Where I had come from, this would have been a subtly intimate gesture on her part, but knowing Marie, I was not sure
it meant anything. The fact is, though, I also knew — from the
source — that there was trouble between Chrétien and Marie.
He had accused her of too much flirtation and knew he was
in stiff competition with the older serious womanizers lurking
every evening around the card table, including André.

But Marie herself was not without guile or her own defenses.

The dentist named Eugène, who was still in residence, seemed
to have developed an infatuation with Marie. He was much older,
perhaps thirty-five or forty to her mere eighteen years, but he
was clearly taken; you could see his eyes following her when
she tripped across the terrace to select her table in the shade.
He would watch as she arranged herself to wait for the delivery
of her citron pressé. He watched as she exited with her bathing apparel, headed for her place on the rocks. Once or twice, I
noticed that when she was sunbathing, he would find an excuse
to stroll out the path beyond the restaurant with his little dog,
Piti, his hands clasped behind his back. He would circle the cove
and select a spot under the Genoese watchtower. I realized later

that he could probably see her from across the cove stretched out topless in the hot light.

Eugène liked me, too, and would sometimes corner me and tell me about his life in Lyon. He would describe in loving detail the antics of his companion, Piti, his custom of rising early, and his happy weekends with her in the parks and how much she loved to chase balls. He was fond of eating, and like Herr Komandante, would arrive early and sit with an aperitif, waiting for his soup, watching for the grand entrance of Marie. Sometimes he would manage to have a few words with her at the bar, although she was often surrounded at these times by other adoring males.

One day I saw them walking together out toward the tower. Piti was prancing ahead of them, tail on high. Eugène was carrying himself stiffly and formally, and Marie was stepping along with her deerlike, balletic walk, shoulders back, her hips swaying subtly. They were gone for two hours or more, and when they came back she had her hand crooked in his arm. He held himself uncomfortably, his left arm half-raised across his lower chest and repressing a proud smile, as if he had just won an important athletic victory and was approaching an adoring public.

Marie was free with her hands and body; she would often reach out and touch you while she prattled on, she was not averse to squeezing past you in a doorway, and she would sometimes lean close and press her breasts against your arm if she was looking at something over your shoulder. But none of this meant that she was particularly attracted to you, she just liked to be appreciated — she liked to be liked. This was the behavior that enraged Chrétien, who would fly into fits of jealousy and sometimes corner me in the kitchen and hold forth confidentially about her loose behavior, not to mention her stiff defenses against his passionate advances.

Out on the island below the tower, she had probably laughed at something Eugène said and leaned her moplike head against his shoulder; maybe she had tousled his hair or grabbed his knee to make a point. She would often take the arm of men and women when she walked, but in his mind, this freedom must have been layered with great meaning. He actually believed she favored him, and he must have invited her to join him at dinner that evening, and she must have accepted, because we were instructed to lay two settings at the dentist's table in the corner.

Eugène arrived early, as was his custom, and instructed Piti to lie down under the table. He had washed and put on a fresh shirt, one of his new ones — barely out of the box, I would say. He wore pressed slacks and leather sandals over neat brown socks, and he sat down complacently for once, with an almost self-satisfied look. Chrétien brought him his usual kir, not suspecting that Monsieur le Dentiste was to dine that evening with his own girlfriend. Eugène was ever so gracious with Chrétien that evening, joking and free, and not quite understanding, or perhaps unconsciously suppressing the fact, that Chrétien and Marie were a couple (more or less).

A group had gathered at the bar: Maggs, a man from the town named Pierre, and a young woman named Circe, who had worked as a waitress at the café the season before. They were collected in a loose circle, laughing and throwing back their heads like barking dogs. And then, in the doorway, Marie made her entrance.

As she often would do, she moved in out of the light and stood framed by the door for a second, waiting for everyone to look up and notice. She wore her green capri pants, a tight black blouse with deep décolletage, silver earrings, and many silver necklaces and bracelets. As if in surprise, she spotted the troupe of her friends, and made for them, light-footed. Halfway across the room, she saw the dentist.

"*Oh là*," she said, "*Eugène, mon ami, comment vas tu?*" and detoured toward his table.

He rose to greet her, but before he had even straightened himself, she reached the table, leaned across, kissed him on each cheek, and carried on to the bar.

I saw the sunbeam fade from his face. He sat down, busied himself with his drink, broke a morsel of bread from the basket and fed it to Piti, and then spent the next few minutes pretending not to notice the happy throng at the bar.

Chrétien served him his dinner not ever suspecting the assignation so closely missed.

Along with many of the other men around the café, I had also seen le Baron eyeing Marie. One night he dropped out of the card game and joined her at the bar. Chrétien was still serving the last diners, but he seemed to make a point of finding odd jobs for himself around the counter, glancing over frequently at their little tête-à-tête. Le Baron's searchlight eyes were shining more brightly that evening, I thought, and he was fixing Marie with that lowered-head stare he assumed whenever he spoke with anyone who interested him.

Out on the rocks that Friday afternoon I asked Marie if she knew le Baron. "I saw him talking to you the other night," I said.

"You think he is a big criminal, don't you? Chrétien told me that."

"I don't know," I said. "I've heard that from one source, but Micheline says he's from a rich coal mining family in Belgium. An industrialist or something. Lots of money."

"I do not trust him either," she said. "I caught him looking me over. He makes me nervous."

"I think he just likes younger people," I said. "He engaged me in conversation one evening, asked me all about New York. He looked at me the same way."

"He claims to know of my mother and father. Or at least their writing," she said.

"What does he think?"

"I don't think he likes their politics very much."

I told her I thought it strange to have a type like him out here in the middle of nowhere. "If he were in Nice, or Cannes, you wouldn't think twice," I said. "But out here — out in the maquis, with all those feral pigs and peasants."

"Micheline told me there is a strange, one-eyed guard out on his property. A mute who only grunts at people and limps. Also a big dog. A mastiff," she said.

She leaned over my knee again as a shadowy form spirited out from a crevice and disappeared with some fish innards — an octopus, I think.

"My parents, they are coming back next weekend. I will ask them. They know everything. If he's a big enough crook they will know. Or just ask Micheline again. She knows him quite well. She knows the house."

"Micheline goes out there?" I asked.

"Of course, you don't know that? She used to go out often, she and Jean-Pierre. Then just Micheline."

She glanced up to see if I was listening.

"I think they had an affair," she whispered.

That at least helped to explain Micheline's curious caginess whenever I asked her about le Baron. It did not explain how he got so rich, though, and why he had chosen to live such an isolated life. It always seemed to me a great irony that he would dress so formally out here in this casual little outpost — paisley cravats and pressed trousers, starched shirts, expensive Belgian linen suit, or a houndstooth sport coat with a hint of Savile Row.

"What do you think of that?" she asked.

"What, that they had an affair?"

"Yes."

I hesitated. It was interesting. But that kind of thing was no longer shocking to me. I was more concerned with le Baron's story at that point.

"You are such a cowboy," she said before I could answer, "so polite and innocent."

Then, suddenly, she kissed me.

"There," she said. "Cowboy."

"No cowboy," I spluttered into her cheek.

"American cowboy," she said. "Horse."

She kissed me again and then tried to push me forward into the water, down into the jeweled sea tangle, among the darting predators and the octopus and the fish scales. As I fell, I turned and grabbed her wrist and dragged her down with me. She fell on top of me, and then, struggling, she grabbed my head, pushed me under, and held me there.

She was strong for such a small sprite, but she brought me up, kissed me quickly, and then pushed me under once more.

"Water horse," she shouted. "Cowboy who cannot swim."

I managed to break free, grabbed her waist, lifted her, and skidded her out into the deeper water, and she sank beneath the surface and didn't come up. Only a silent line of bubbles, the gulls circling above. I could see her down there, a shimmering, glowing form in the blue-green shallows, so I swam over and lifted her out. This time she lay in my arms, limp, not breathing, her mouth open, feigning death. Her tiny silver crucifix was skewed from her chest and lay gleaming against her right shoulder, her dark wet hair was flattened at her temples. Full lips, high cheekbones, she was a Gallic beauty, softened by a thousand years of civilization. But she sprang to life, grabbed my head, pushed me down again, and held me there for a long time, her small hands tightening on the back of my neck every time I tried to rise.

I too came up dead.

"*Mortu?*" she asked in dialect. "Dead?"

"*Sì.*"

"Then I will kiss the frog prince to bring him back to life," she said.

There followed a soft, evolving kiss.

This was hardly the embrace of a fairy queen or a virginal Catholic teenager. It was the practiced kiss of a Parisian sophisticate.

Just before dinner that night two tall, dark-eyed men carrying instrument cases came in the back door of the kitchen and asked if Micheline was around. They were serious types, without the usual ebullience of island people, and once I had directed them to the dining room where Micheline was talking with some clients, they walked off without so much as a nod.

"Who were they?" I asked Vincenzo.

"Those are the gypsy musicians. Micheline picked them up in the market yesterday. They're going to play tonight."

The two men were directed to the nook beside the bar — an area usually used only for drinks or light fare. Chrétien was instructed to lay out two settings and once they were in place, Micheline brought them a bottle of vermentinu from one of the Cap Corse vineyards. They drank sullenly, without grace, and talked quietly to each other in some dialect I couldn't understand.

All that day Jean-Pierre had been preparing a *stifatu*. This was a specialty dish, a roll of stuffed meats, prepared from a mix of goat and lamb combined with herbs from the maquis and in some cases locally trapped blackbirds. It was served with grated cheese and was rather time-consuming to prepare. Spotting it on the menu, the regular diners had been ordering the dish, and we were down to the last serving when Micheline scurried in and announced that the gypsies had ordered that particular plate.

"Too late," Jean-Pierre said. "I'm just about to send out the last order to one of Chrétien's tables."

"Well, send it to the gypsies. I will tell Chrétien to say there is no more of that dish."

"Why should we serve two itinerant gypsies with limited palates one of our finest dishes? Why waste it?" he said.

"Why not?" she spit. They were about to have one of their rows, I could see, and so I quietly retreated with a load of dirty dishes and began washing. I could hear the argument from the scullery, but I noticed later that the gypsies got their stifatu.

In spite of the unpleasantness in the back room, out in the dining room and on the terrace things were livening up. A lot of local people had come out along with the usual card sharks, and many bottles of muscat and local rosés were opened and served, and the talk back and forth between the tables was loud and riotous. The place was full; I had vast amounts of dishes and silverware pouring in at me, and had to work furiously to keep up with the flow. I was drenched from the work, and the stone floor of the scullery was slick with grease and bits of rice and peas and fish bones. Toward the end, as I was finishing up the pans, I could hear the music start up, the whiny, sad sound of a gypsy violin.

Vincenzo came in with my usual glass of marc.

"Come out soon," he said. "They're very good."

When I went back to my cabine to get some dry clothes I saw a couple in an embrace up on the promontory. They broke apart quickly when they saw me pass and turned to face the dull red glow of the last of daylight over the western horizon. I tried not to look too closely, but the woman had the same build as Maggs, and the man she was with was a short island type, not her tall, rangy husband. I assumed I was mistaken, and when I came back out to go up to the festivities, they were gone.

The gypsies were still running through slower numbers when I finally managed to get out to the terrace. In contrast to the two surly individuals who first appeared, they had now transformed themselves. They played mostly American popular tunes from the 1950s. One played the guitar in the chopped, pulsing style of Django Reinhardt, smiling to show two golden teeth. The other played in the jazz fiddle style of Django's partner Stephane Grappelli, bowing forward at the low notes and rocking back on his heels, head to the sky, on the higher notes. When I got to the terrace, they were working through a slow, Eastern European, gypsy-like lament, the guitar walking along rhythmically, the violin wheeling up to higher registers and then slowly sinking in a sad minor key to its lowest possible range. People at the tables were listening, still finishing desserts and coffee. Others had had their tables cleared and had pushed back their chairs to get a better view of the performers. As the last of the coffees and local ratafias were served, the music began to heat up. A young couple from the town finally could not sit still any longer, pushed their table aside and began to dance. This inspired another couple, then another. And then Micheline eyed me and swung her head to Chrétien, indicating that we should help the customers move some tables aside — something we would do periodically when some pick-up dance band came out from the town. Chrétien and I set to work and cleared a circle in the center of the terrace, and even before we finished our work, people jumped in.

The island women wore wide, flouncy skirts and peasant blouses in an outmoded style from the 1950s, and the men were dressed in dark trousers and white collared shirts or tight jerseys, although there were a few older locals there who still wore baggy pants, a beret, and a striped sailor's jersey. Some of the younger people danced the jitterbug, but during the slower numbers they all swept into one another's arms and danced in the old *apache* style, leaning into each other, cheek to cheek, legs moving together in a quickstep. The guitar pulsed steadily along with a chug-a-chug dancer's heartbeat, and the fiddle wound through the night air, jumping in a jagged swing melody from time to time, and surging out over the harbor. It was a still night, a moist night, and I daresay the older townspeople lingering along the promenade that ran along the harbor beside the town square could hear the violin complaining and whining as it shimmered across the bay and mixed with the soft lap of the waters on the rocks.

The gypsies went on for over an hour with no break, and all the while we pulled big pitchers of beer, cracked open bottles of champagne and prosecco and a sparkling variety of local muscat, and wove among the dancers with laden trays of drink orders. The music chopped onward, the gypsies playing some of the older popular American numbers — "St. Louis Woman" and the "Beale Street Blues." The Chinese lanterns we had strung around the terrace swayed with the rhythm, chairs tipped over, people sat along the terrace wall in the hot, humid sea air, and we could hardly keep up with the drink orders. There appeared to be no sign of an end to the evening.

Inside, in the quieter space of the dining room, a few of the regulars, driven indoors by the wild scene on the terrace, were also dancing and drinking, albeit in a far more subdued manner.

Maggs was there, stepping around the cleared floor with Peter in a stylized English manner. Eugène, the dentist, sat at the bar with Herr Komandante, trying to communicate above the noise in whatever common language they could find; Jacquis was inside too, dancing in the apache style with a very sexy woman in a tight skirt and a low-cut blouse.

Marie was out on the terrace dancing a hot caper with a couple of local boys who had seen her in the town periodically. She was wearing a red skirt, cut close at the hips but flared just below her knees, and she had on a tight, striped sailor's jersey, cut square at the neck, and big hooped earrings and dark little ballet slippers.

Every time I would go out to serve a table she was there with a new partner, swinging her hips, twirling under his arm, swaying back, and then reuniting with her partner, cheek to cheek, only to break away again and spin off into a twirl. She put them all to shame, old and young alike, with her speed and her lithe turns and dips.

After the events of the afternoon, I felt a little resentment seeing her out there with questionable local toughs from the village, but I was too busy to dance with her anyway. In any case, this sentiment was nothing compared with the green eye of jealousy that was piercing the night from Chrétien. Every time he went out on the terrace with a tray he glared at her. At one point, she floated past him in a slow number, cheek to cheek, and for a second perceived his venomous glare. She turned quickly and spun into her partner's arms, and the two of them twirled off, their bodies molded together.

It occurred to me that the young town boy was lucky that Chrétien was a civilized graduate student in philosophy at the Sorbonne whose parents had a big flat on the Champs Elysées. Up in the isolated hill towns, incidents of this sort still begat knife fights. As it was, he retreated to the bar and was downing a glass of fiery marc when I came in for more orders.

"Not worth it," he muttered. "Not a chance. She's a tease. A mindless, egotistical little tease. A nanny goat coming into estrus but not yet ready to receive the male. I'm through with her."

I tried to find the French idiom for "there are many fish in the sea," but I couldn't come up with it.

At one point, later in the night, I saw le Baron sitting at the bar with Max. He was dressed as always in his clean linen suit, and he had turned to face the dance floor. I noticed that he was eyeing Maggs, who was at this point dancing a slower number with Peter and looking rather bored, I thought.

"Busy night, isn't it?" le Baron said to me when I passed.

I agreed and carried on, and when I passed by him again, he said, "I hope you'll get some time to dance. There are some pretty little dark-eyed Corsican girls out there for you, no?"

I laughed and carried on. "No time so far," I said.

Slowly, the night began to calm. The gypsies took a break and sat on the terrace wall drinking beer and smoking privately. Micheline went over and sat with them for a while sharing a cigarette, and I saw them eyeing her in a way I didn't like when she left them and walked off across the terrace. She had on her Moroccan striped trousers, masses of clanky jewelry, and she looked good that night, flushed, with coppery skin and her fall of uncontrollable hair.

One of the gypsies said something out of the corner of his mouth to his partner as he watched her walk away, and the other smiled and snickered through his nose.

After a break they picked up again but started playing slower numbers. The dancers clung together now, circling the floor as the music swept along — pale rose petals, floating across the stone terrace under the half-light of the Chinese lanterns.

Le Baron came out from the interior and danced with Micheline in a formal, graceful style, holding her around the waist with his left arm crooked, his back ramrod straight. He looked down on her kindly from his upright position — even lovingly, you might say if you were the type to read significance into superficialities. But the number wound down, then ceased, and she broke away and went back to work. Five minutes later I saw le Baron dancing with Marie. He moved with the same solicitous formality, the same glowing look of kindly love, chatting on with her as they ranged around the terrace, feet stepping delicately. She didn't miss a beat, and she threw back her head and laughed at something he said, arching her body into his, and then spinning off into one of her perfect twirls. Their feet moved gracefully together in a patterned foxtrot with an airy lightness, as if they were not touching the heavy stone of the terrace.

The music slowed even more, and then the gypsies played "Good Night Ladies," and the little tripping circlets of the guitar runs spiraled upward and outward, and the violin complained, and then they segued into an apparent favorite for the evening, "Red Sails in the Sunset," and then it was over, and the people slipped off arm in arm down the causeway into the darkness.

We cleared the tables, straightened the chairs, and then extinguished the lanterns and we were suddenly alone under that black, star-pierced curtain of the Corsican night.

chapter seven # The Barefoot Contessa

Marie and her tutor never worked out very well. She was supposed to meet with him twice a day, once in the morning and then again in the afternoon — at the unheard-of hour of two o'clock, when the sun was at its hottest and the air at its thickest, and the café and the town square were emptied of all life. I would often see Marie and the tutor sitting together at a shaded table on the verandah: Giancarlo, the professor, in his gray suit and tie, Marie in as few clothes as possible, swinging her leg restlessly and allowing her eyes to stray over the landscape beyond the harbor while her would-be teacher fixed her with his hawkish glare.

"*Oui, oui, oui, je comprends, je comprends, oui,*" I could hear her saying impatiently.

"You understand what?" Giancarlo would insist, "To understand is to acquire. What is the origin of the word *understand*? It is to stand beneath, to take in mind an idea, a phrase, the depth of a human soul, and if, in fact, you take it in mind, then it is a part of you. Therefore, I wish you to tell what part you have taken in, please? I do not observe any empirical evidence of comprehension on your part, mademoiselle."

And on it would go. Giancarlo would back up, analyze every word and phrase in every possible combination and permutation, and then, little by little, move on to the next possible interpretation of the next idea. He was driving her crazy. But Chrétien found him intriguing and would sometimes join them, arguing over the connotations of certain phrases, citing various interpretations from various linguistic authorities. Marie would excuse herself to go to the bathroom during these sessions and then go to the beach. Giancarlo would by that time be so engaged in a discussion of Bergson's theories of duration and simultaneity that he would fail to notice that he had lost his pupil. And so it went, until finally, whenever he was free, Chrétien would take the place of Marie. They argued about everything: the doctrines of the church, intuitive knowledge, the question of the stream of consciousness, Sartre's being and nothingness, as well as the question of Gide's *acte gratuit* and the nature of free will, a subject on which Giancarlo's pupil was perhaps the ultimate local authority.

At the end of June, Marie's parents came down for a few days, intending to take her with them to visit an auntie who had a villa for the season near Vence. They stayed on for the long weekend, but unlike the other guests — many of whom had no particular passions other than to eat and drink and relax in the sun — they grew restless and were forever walking into town to the public phone offices to put through calls to their respective news bureaus.

I saw Simone out on the terrace one afternoon, her flowery muumuu lifted above her knees, head back to the sun, half-asleep and yawning periodically.

"Tired?" I asked as I passed her table.

"Yes," she said. "Tired of nothing to do."

I moved a few chairs and picked up a journal someone had left, and read a few passages about popular music in Paris.

"What are you doing out here, anyway?" Simone asked. "You're a student someplace?"

There followed the usual small talk. And when I expressed an interest in writing, she jokingly advised me against it.

"Look at us," she said, "dogged by everyone. If you write, someone will hate you."

I told her about the interesting stories I had been picking up here on the island about local resistance fighters.

"Yes, but don't believe it. You do know that after liberation, all of a sudden half the males in France were in the resistance?"

"I don't believe. But the stories are entertaining."

"That's it. All entertainment. Except for some. Some are too real. Then you try to tell it and they try to shut you up. That's the job of the state, isn't it? Keep the press quiet."

She began to spin out a long story that had recently broken about what some journalists were calling a police "massacre" that had taken place in Paris back in October. The Algerians in Paris, long oppressed and living under a curfew, had turned out on the streets in huge numbers one night to protest the curfew. Police responded accordingly and put down the demonstration.

"Only they were killing protestors in the process," she said. "Papon and his troupe."

Maurice Papon was the Paris chief of police, a man hated by the left and a Nazi sympathizer who would later be convicted for his role in the deportation of French Jews from the Bordeaux area.

Simone's story astonished me. I think I had been there that night.

I was coming back to my room after dinner and was talking to a friend of mine on the phone in a booth at the end of the Boulevard Saint-Michel, near the Seine, when I was engulfed by a sea of Algerians surging down the boulevard toward the river. I remembered the incident distinctly because this was the first time I had ever seen Algerian women, and because they were ululating in loud, ringing cries that filled the night air. I described the scene to my friend as it was occurring, and he became very agitated and told me to get down to the nearest Métro and take the first train, no matter where it was going.

I stepped out of the booth and was instantly swept along by the crowd. No one seemed to resent my presence, in fact my memory of it is that they were having a good time. The women were waving their hands in the air and chirping and shouting and laughing, and I was carried along by this great sweeping tide to the station by the river. I had no choice; there were so many, and they were packed so tightly, you had to move with them. My inclination was to stay and watch, but my friend had been so agitated that I took his advice, fought through the current to the corner, and ducked down into the station.

I couldn't be certain, but I thought that above the roar of the first train I had heard gunshots.

Simone was shocked by this story.

"You were there?" she asked, horrified. "You actually saw them? Do you know that the police killed maybe as many as one hundred people that night, right at that spot? They threw the bodies into the Seine. A massacre, but it was completely covered up. I don't know whether you remember the news the next day. They reported the riot and little else. People with information — witnesses like you — they were ignored. Police wouldn't talk to the press to corroborate. Of course they wouldn't. Why should they? You kill people and then throw them in the river, you're not going to admit it to the press. We really don't know the whole truth yet. But there are people working to find out. Still, no authorities are talking, but there are some who say de Gaulle knew all about this pending demonstration and let Papon have his way. He was saving himself with a bow to the right, they say. You know, there was genuine fear that there was going to be a right-wing coup d'état. Someone had to give the right a little breathing room is the theory. So de Gaulle, he looks the other way. Let it be."

She went on to spin out stories of the big news breaks in Paris that she and her husband had been dealing with over the past winter. It was indeed an exciting year in France, with the forces of the right-wing generals and the police, who supported the European Algerian colonials, opposing the left, which supported independence for Algeria. I was surprised to realize how many incidents I had witnessed.

I had gotten used to the dreaded predawn pounding on doors of the cheap rooms around Place Monge where I often stayed, and the shakedowns for proper identity cards, plus a few incidents of police brutality inflicted upon my left-wing student friends. And one night that winter, staying with an au pair friend at a good address on the Left Bank, I was awakened by the *thud* of a predawn explosion. That night the right wing, the OAS, had tried to blow up Jean-Paul Sartre's apartment, which was located just down the street from where I was staying.

Many of my friends in Paris were intensely political, some actively involved with the FLN, the National Liberation Front, and every night at the café near Saint-Placide they would get into intense arguments over Algeria — or over anything political, it seemed to me. You could not enter a WC in those years without reading through political graffiti advocating one cause or another. Most of my student friends, French and German alike, had very little allegiance to their countries. "We're for Europe," they would argue.

All this was in sharp contrast to the detached life I had been leading in the green and budding suburbs of the East Coast of the United States, where the biggest concern was to find the next party.

"I heard from Marie that you are interested in this man they call le Baron?" Simone said.

I tried to seem indifferent but admitted that I was.

"Sort of," I said. "He's interesting. He's so different from anyone else around here. More like a type you'd see in Saint-Tropez."

"He *is* the type you see in Saint-Tropez," she said.

I asked if she knew anything about him.

"No, only his sort," she said. "Old money. Too much time on his hands."

"But was it old money? Or did he get it some other way?"

I told her Fabrizio's story.

"Not impossible," she said. "But then some of those old monarchist types — if that's what he is — Hitler would just put them under house arrest. Some of them helped the underground. A few got caught and executed. But I never heard of anyone from old Belgian families actively helping Nazis."

"But couldn't he have just been helping himself?" I said.

She began to laugh. "Maybe. Why not?" she said.

At the end of the weekend, Marie and her family left for Calvi to get the ferry back to Nice. They took Giancarlo with them and paid his bill.

After the dance and their falling-out, Chrétien purposely stayed away from Marie on the day she left, even though most of the staff came out to kiss her goodbye. She would be back in ten days, but without her somehow the café lacked some of its decoration. She was like some exotic animal that lived around the estate grounds and emerged from the forest at dusk, to the delight of her watchers.

For a while after Marie left, Chrétien would corner me on the terrace with complaints about her absence. He seemed to be attempting to convince himself that it was a good thing that they were no longer together. I had to listen over and over again to his descriptions of his tender nights with her and her earnest declarations of love and admiration for him. "And then what?" he said. "Nothing. A few kisses, a few intimate caresses, and it is over. Go back to your own room. *Finito. Basta. Noli me tangere.*"

He slapped the bar and spread out his palms to the world at large, raising his arms. "*Ma che?* — what can you do? It is finished."

"Good," I said.

"What do you mean good?" he asked loudly. "Why good? You want her?"

"No," I said. I did not tell him about our wrestling match in the water.

"She loves you. I can see it," he said. "She eyes you when you are not watching. She watches you when you come out with that broom and go around pretending to sweep the floor and clear dishes. You are to be her next victim. Be careful."

"Will you pray for me?" I asked.

He fell into one of his paroxysms of laughter.

"But of course," he said. "But it is not necessary. She will pray for you herself if you get too close. She will tell you she is going to pray for you. She will tell you she is going to go into a nunnery and pray for you if you persist with her.

"Catholic!" he shouted suddenly to no one in particular. "Theist! Believer in myths and fairy tales, fabrications to hold the worker in thrall to the anvil and the plow. I tell her there should be no religions in the world. She asks God to forgive me, so I challenge God to strike me dead. I shout at the sky and he doesn't strike. 'He will,' she says. 'Later.' So I tell her that if there is some god up there he's a creep. She is better than God, far more beautiful, and not as cruel. 'Stop,' she says. 'Don't go on.' She is in shock. 'What can I possibly mean, better than God? Nothing is better than God.' So I ask her, would she go out and kill people with plagues and wars, would she cause innocent babies to suffer and then die, would she purposely allow those with no hope of salvation — animals, for instance — to suffer? 'Stop!' she says. 'No more.' She stuffs her ears.

"But it's all a joke, you see. She's not a real Catholic. She doesn't believe in the Church any more than I do. Ask her parents. This is a new thing with her. Her parents are good atheists. She was never confirmed, never went to Mass until she was fourteen, and then she went on her own, against her parents' will."

"Well, that explains it," I said. "It will pass."

"Maybe. But why could it not have passed in the bedroom during an embrace?"

One afternoon toward the end of that week, I saw Chrétien leering from the terrace, crouching half-hidden by the verandah walls.

"Look what's coming," he said when I joined him.

Out on the road, three people were approaching: a young red-haired man with glasses, a dark, short-haired woman in her late twenties or early thirties, and behind them, striding along, a voluptuous young woman in a white shift with tanned skin and a fall of chestnut hair, barefoot.

"It is the Barefoot Contessa coming here," Chrétien said. "What a beauty. The Queen of Night."

"More like a *contadina*," I said, "a peasant, coming in from the fields."

"*Non, non, non,*" Chrétien said. "Not a contadina, not at all, she is from a good family — nobility. A long line of Italian dukes, conceived in the night gardens beside the moonlit fountains of Tuscany. Look at the way she walks. The peasant waddles when she comes in from the field, tired from work, carrying the heavy-fruited baskets. Look at the forceful, straightforward stride of this young noblewoman. She may be a contessa, but she is lit within by burning animal passions, you can tell."

"Maybe," I said.

"*Non, non,* for sure," Chrétien said. "She has the fire of the ages, not yet extinguished by the unforgiving Protestant govern-ess who taught her English. Not at all."

And all the while, as Chrétien prattled on with his inventions, the troupe approached. They were carrying packs and bags with them, and since there would be no ferry for several days, it was clear that they were intending to stay at the auberge.

They came onward, the two in the lead weighted with bags, the contessa traveling light, a small satchel slung over her left shoulder.

Chrétien was electrified.

"Come on," he said. "Back into the bar and the kitchen. We must appear indifferent. We are not sure there are rooms. But of course, we will make arrangements in the end. The contessa will be grateful."

The threesome turned out to be Parisian, and hardly Italian nobility. The young, neatly dressed man was a cousin of the two women, who were sisters: Clotilde and Karen. They had been traveling together since late winter, hitchhiking and taking trains and ferries; they had come out here, as many did, to escape the scene on the Riviera.

True to form, when they asked for rooms, Chrétien told them

we were full. Then he called me out from the kitchen and held a long discussion with me as to the situation with the German family in Room 6. There was no German family in Room 6. In fact, there was no Room 6 — there were just rooms, unnumbered and most of them empty at that point, but I caught his drift and played along.

"The steward here says he is not sure, a family of Germans may be leaving today, but we will find out from the patron, who is off fishing at the moment. In the meantime — please. Sit. Have something to drink."

How he intended to get out of this lie, I did not know. Jean-Pierre and Micheline were enjoying their midafternoon rendez-vous in the next room and would soon be out for their afternoon coffee.

Chrétien brought over two glasses of beer and a citron pressé, and with uncommon flourish delivered the citron pressé to Karen, the contessa.

"And for the belle madame . . ." he said as he set down the glass.

"Thanks," the contessa said with a slangy Parisian intonation.

She had close-set brown eyes, a large Italianate mouth, and a fine row of white teeth but was gat-toothed, an imperfection that made her all the more interesting, I thought.

I was busying myself with the other tables nearby.

"Are you a Brit?" the older sister asked, speaking in English.

"American," I said.

"Interesting," she said. "Not many Americans here in the south."

"I know, that's why I like it."

"On the run?" she asked.

I wasn't sure what she meant and explained innocently that I was a student in Paris, just here for the summer. Nothing about the American draft service trying to catch up with me.

"Good place to hide if, perhaps, the military wanted you," she said.

We fell into conversation, and I learned that they were White Russians whose grandparents had come to Paris in the 1920s. The two sisters were now apparently making up for their lost youths in a Bohemian sort of way. They had left Paris in February and hitchhiked all through western Spain, and then they started north as the weather warmed and crossed the Pyrenees near Saint-Jean-de-Luz, hiking from time to time on mountain trails used by smugglers and shepherds. Then they descended through the villages of the foothills and began hitching across the Côte d'Azur. They picked up their younger cousin Laurent in Nice, where they had spent a few weeks, and then came out to Calvi.

Laurent had curly, carrot-colored hair and wore heavy tortoiseshell glasses that somehow jarred with his coloring. He was about Marie's age and very interested in clothes. He wore a clean white shirt, denim trousers, leather sandals, and had rolled the sleeves of his shirt halfway up his forearms and folded the cuffs neatly. He was forever arranging his hair. Like Marie he was a student at a lycée, but he was not at all afraid of his upcoming baccalaureate, which he would have to face the following year.

In time Jean-Pierre and Micheline emerged from their bed, and as was their custom, shuffled, bleary-eyed, through the dining room to the kitchen to prepare coffee, paying no attention to the new troupe in the bar.

Chrétien followed them in, and after a few minutes emerged

and went over to the table where I was chatting with the new arrivals.

"I have good news for you," he said. "It seems that, unbeknownst to me, the German family left this morning, and the room is in fact free, and so if you would permit, the steward and I will assist you with your belongings."

He made the pretense of a bow. "Please . . ." he said, extending his arm toward the narrow, dark stairwell that led up to the second floor. Knowing Chrétien, I didn't think his ruse was working very well. They must have thought him a fool. He snatched up the contessa's pack and, carrying it in front of his chest with two hands as if it were precious cargo, mounted the stairs and led the way through the hallway to a big room with a dormer overlooking the harbor. I followed sheepishly, playing along.

The room was wide and airy, with a creaky double bed and a cot. It had peeling yellow wallpaper, a sink and bidet by the back wall, and a rickety armoire in one corner. I spotted an earwig struggling to climb up the sink wall and brushed it away.

"Is it to your liking?" Chrétien asked, addressing the contessa.

"It's OK," she said. "We'll take it."

"But for me?" Laurent asked. "Where am I to sleep?"

This began a discussion as to whether Laurent would be sharing the room with his cousins or would have quarters of his own, and this in turn, to keep up the ruse, required that Chrétien descend and check the books to see if a room was available, which he knew perfectly well there was.

Karen went over and threw open the windows, allowing a blast of fresh sea air to flow in. She stood in the breeze in her light shift, shaking out her hair with both hands.

"Beautiful, no?" she said to her sister.

"Compared to where we've been, I'll say."

"I don't fancy that infested cot," Laurent said.

"It will do . . ." Clotilde said to him.

"No, it will not do. I must have a better bed, as you know," Laurent said.

"We'll see," said Karen.

Chrétien returned with more "good news." The single room was available. He indicated to me through a sign that I should lead the young gentleman to his new quarters, which I did.

A few days after the arrival of la Contessa and her family, Pierrot asked if I would like to go back into the maquis to see his father.

"He liked meeting you," he said. "He wants to tell you more about the Nazis."

It was good to get away from the coast for a change. We motored up on the winding roads and clattered through empty, stony villages. At one point, an old crone stood at a turning, and when we slowed to make the turn, she cocked her thumb and forefinger like a pistol and pretended to shoot at us.

"Local *pazza*," Pierrot shouted back at me over his shoulder. "Crazy but harmless."

In time we came to the track leading up to the meadow, and we began weaving through the dense vegetation and the thick-scented air of the maquis. Partly because I spent most of my time on the coast, I was more aware of the diversity of plants and birdsong in that particular little valley. We had been climbing through the various levels of maquis, first broom and myrtle, then a section dominated by arbutus and briar, and eventually an area of a mixed, shrubby understory interspersed with chestnut trees, which provided one of the staples of Corsican cuisine. Chestnuts are pounded into flour for breads; they are used in a flan; they are mixed with stews; and they are distilled into the uniquely flavored aperitif, averna.

From time to time as we walked, lizards spirited across our path, so fast you could hardly be sure you'd seen them at all, and birds were twittering all around us in the thickets: Cetti's warblers, chaffinches, thrushes, and wood pigeons. I could hear also the tapping of woodpeckers and a whole host of unidentifiable whistles, chirps, and chirrups.

It was another typically hot day, with the sound of cicadas ringing out as a figured accompaniment to the chattering of the birds, and hardly so much as a remembered whisper of wind stirred the air. At one point, Pierrot turned off the track and followed a narrow trail to a clear spring that bubbled up from a cleft in the rocks. He knelt and drank from it, cupping the waters in his hands, and then splashed himself, sweeping his wet hands back through his hair.

"Safe to drink?" I asked.

He looked at me in a way that indicated that he did not understand the intent of my question. I cupped my hands and sucked up the cool, mineral-rich water, and then washed my face.

We hiked on, Pierrot in the lead, his battered, down-at-heel espadrilles slapping the ground as he carefully picked his way through the rocks. This was the backcountry of the Corsican foothills, the short, steep valleys that led up to the higher peaks. Although it seemed hard to believe with the great white towers of the higher peaks showing themselves from time to time above the lower peaks, this was one of the least mountainous areas of

Corsica. The serious heights occurred farther south, between Corte and Ajaccio.

The wild interior of Corsica supports some of Europe's last endemic species, the Corsican nuthatch, for example, which lived higher up in the forest of Corsican pines — themselves a unique subspecies. The Tyrrhenian wall lizard could be found in these parts, and in some of the lower levels there were still remnant populations of Hermann's tortoise, which was extinct on the European mainland. Best known of all, in the peaks around us there were mouflon, a native Corsican sheep with great, curling horns.

Just as the track began to shrink down to a mere trail, Pierrot bent quickly and snatched up a wildflower with many bright yellow petals, like an aster. Suddenly the close air was filled with the smell of camphor.

"Smell this," he said.

The odor was so strong you could feel it on your tongue.

"If you get bitten by a mosquito, you rub this on the bite. No more itch. Good for cuts and scratches, too."

When we finally got to the ruins, Fabrizio was off someplace, maybe chasing after a stray donkey. We sat in his chairs for a while and drank some of his bad wine and ate a few figatelli and hunks of bread from the baguettes that Pierrot had brought along. In time the old man came lumbering up the track, leading a younger donkey. Pierrot cut him some bread and sausage while the two of them chatted in dialect.

"How do you like your work?" Fabrizio asked after a few minutes.

I told him it was OK. Not too hard, and I had enough time to take off and poke around during the day.

"I don't know what it's like now," Fabrizio said. "But that place used to have a bad reputation. Set off like that from the village, men used to take womens out there. Did you know that, Pierrot? Did you know that that used to be a place to pick up loose womens?"

"No Papé, I didn't know that. But I heard that. But now it is different. Jean-Pierre and Micheline. They're from Paris."

The old man snorted and drank off his glass.

I saw a hawk slip out into the clearing and suddenly bank and dive down into the brush at the edge of the thickets. It came up with a small mammal in its claws.

"Good catch," Fabrizio said.

Pierrot grunted.

For some reason neither of them seemed inclined to talk much. By that time I had been hearing so many stories about the old man that I was anxious to ask him to verify some of the rumors, but I didn't know how to begin.

When I first met Fabrizio, I took him for another old countryman with a briarwood pipe and a traditional wide-brimmed, battered fedora. But now I noticed that he did seem to have a knowing, wise fatigue in his eyes. All the tales of the resistance and his role as a go-between could have been true. Finally, just to make conversation, I think, he asked me again if I was getting along at Jean-Pierre's.

I said again that I was getting on quite well, only this time I added a long story about Maggs and the war and the Jewish resistance in Warsaw, and how I had met le Baron and how he had told me he knew some people from my town back in America who had worked smuggling Jewish children across the border near Perpignan.

"Le Baron met them, you say?" he asked.

I said yes, somewhere in one of the villages or camps north of Marseille.

He grunted. "I didn't think he was over that way," he said to himself.

"Did you know le Baron during the war?" I asked.

"He used to come up here," Fabrizio said. "Someone over by Monticello was hiding him. They took him up into the mountains from there, and we didn't see him for a few months. Then after the Germans pulled out, he lived down there behind Ile Rousse somewhere. He went back to France after that, but returned here after the war. That's when I got to know him. He used to hunt boar up here, him and some other rich people. Big parties, all dressed up. There was two kinds of resistance, you see. One in Nice and Marseille and Bordeaux. And then here. Here it was different. Back there, in France, everybody is fighting everybody else, communists, Gaullists, British. Out here, single-minded. All grudges forgotten. Only one big vendetta to carry out."

"What was that?"

"Kill fascists."

He grunted again and nodded to himself. "Wait here," he said. He got up slowly and hobbled off to his little stone house and was gone for a while. When he came back he was carrying a bundle of cloth tied with old twine. He set it down at his feet, untied a knot, and spread out a uniform jacket in front of me. It was a Nazi jacket, complete with epaulets, and a collection of various emblems and badges, none of which had any real meaning for me. Folded into the jacket was a small, leather-bound sketchbook. Fabrizio opened it reverently and showed it to me. Inside were refined little ink sketches of plants, birds, and butterflies of the maquis, clearly labeled in German, with the species names in Latin.

"This was Hansi's," he said. "Too bad about old Hansi, right, Pierrot? He wasn't a bad sort."

Pierrot blew out a dismissive sigh.

"That's enough, Papé."

There arose then an energetic stream of curses in dialect from the old man. Then he looked up at me.

"Pierrot here, he is young. He doesn't know what it was like."

"Neither do I," I said.

"You don't want to."

On the way back down the track with Pierrot I asked what his father had done during the war, and who was this Hansi. He told me that Hansi was a German officer and that he was a friend of his father's. He talked about Hansi often, Pierrot said. His father had told him that Hansi was an odd man out, a solitary type who liked nature but was stuck in an unfortunate war. He had no real interest in being a soldier and used to use his free time to wander over the maquis, looking for flowers and birds. He carried a box over his shoulder and would collect plants. He would sketch them and make little notes, and then press the plants between the pages of his notebook. One day while he was out on one of his forays, he accidentally happened upon Fabrizio's compound with its square of ruined buildings. Pierrot said that even though his father could have killed him on the spot and buried him and no one would have known, the two of them fell into conversation and became friends. They shared a general interest in, among other things, the local natural history, about which Fabrizio knew a great deal. Hansi would stop in from time to time and talk about the plants and animals of the countryside. He was especially amused by Fabrizio's collection of donkeys. One day, late in the afternoon, Hansi came walking into the compound. Fabrizio was there with a group of maquisards, and as soon as Hansi appeared in the clearing, they shot him.

"Papé was very upset," Pierrot said. "But he didn't show it, or the others would have suspected him as a collaborator. 'Leave him here,' Papé said. 'I'll bury the bastard.' So after they left, he gave Hansi a proper burial and said some prayers. He hid his emblems and badges and kept his jacket and his notebook."

Down in the square in the town, Pierrot and I shared a beer. The old boules players had gathered — dark lines on either side of the pitch. Hawklike eyes following the flight of the cochonnet, explosive outbursts when the boules landed, jocular sparring and familiar banter.

Gulls and terns skimmed the sand-colored buildings and the red-tiled roofs north of the square, white sails against the searing Mediterranean blue, flights of sparrows in the dust at our feet, women with carriages, young children spinning on the carousel at the west end, shouts and laughter, dog barks, the clank of glasses on china plates, the smell of old beer and cigarettes and dry plane-tree leaves. I was suddenly conscious of a comfortable familiarity here. I felt that I had landed in a place that had a sense of itself, a community forged by deep history rather than intentional town planning.

"Why didn't you get called to go fight in Algeria?" I asked Pierrot. He was about the right age for the army.

He looked over at me sadly. Then he tapped his cheek just below his walleye.

"Maybe you're lucky," I said.

Someone made a good throw on the boule pitch. There was an outburst from the players. Pierrot looked over dully and drank some of his beer. A gull barked. A truck engine fired up in the market stalls. A door slammed.

Knowing how the tide of gossip washed over the Rose Café, I was pretty certain that Pierrot knew I had been hearing stories about his father, but he never offered any information himself. He was a very good island guide when it came to plants and animals and unfounded local rumors, but he never talked much about himself. His mother died when he was young, and he was raised by a maiden aunt who lived in the village of Monticello, just behind Ile Rousse. When he was old enough to make the trip on his own, he started going up into the maquis to stay with his father, and for a while helped him out with his donkey herd and the half-wild cows and pigs that Fabrizio laid claim to. (All the seemingly feral livestock that you would see in the middle of nowhere in the maquis actually belonged to someone.) Pierrot soon grew bored with this way of life and moved down to Ile Rousse, where he managed to get the delivery job for the local baker. People around the café claimed that he was dull-witted and slow and knew very little about his father's activities during the war, save what the old man told him, which he accepted as truth. He accepted everything as truth, they said, still believed in the power of the signadore and was scared of mazzeri, the evil eye, and other occult forces that lingered on in Corsican folklore.

Dull-witted he may well have been, but I noticed that, like his father, Pierrot maintained a store of knowledge about lizards and birds and the uses of local plants.

He finished his beer and said goodbye, and I watched him amble off through the square, occasionally stopping to chat with a few of the men his age. Except for his walleye, he did not seem substantially different from anyone else in the village.

On my way back to work I watched the carousel for a while before I turned down the street that led out to the causeway. Worried mothers watched attentively as their little ones spun in the trapped circle, the horses and zebras rising and falling, rising and falling, the canned calliope music bouncing along.

The carousel slowed and stopped, and released one troupe of riders while the next group selected their chosen mounts. There was a little boy of about three or four who was afraid of the zebra, but his sister, who couldn't have been older than seven or eight herself, leaned over him and escorted him forward; she encouraged him to pat the zebra, and then helped him up onto the saddle. He held on to the post tightly, wide-eyed and terrified. His sister got up behind him and circled him with her arms on the post and leaned forward with her cheek to his. And then they were off.

Up and down, around and around, the high, circling dog-trot waltz rhythm belling along, zebra heads up, horse heads down, appearing and disappearing in the fixed circle, wild eyes, gaping jaws, manes flying, and the innocent faces of laughing children, lost in the joyous absurdity of the circle.

When I left I noticed that the little boy was smiling proudly, tears still glistening in his eyes.

chapter eight Migrants

Migratory birds begin to arrive on the western slopes and headlands of Corsica as early as February, flying north from their wintering grounds in Africa. By March their numbers swell, and by April the maquis is alive with the chirrups and chips and songs of the local nesting birds, including the fluted bell of the blackbird, the explosive little call of the Cetti's warbler, and the various trills, churrs, squeaks, whistles, and buzzes of the linnets and the pipits, and the bee-eaters and buntings.

A pair of house martins began building a nest over a wall lamp earlier in the spring. We saw them first darting through the verandah like half-seen shadows and hovering around the wall lamp where the geckos used to collect at night. Then after a few days, they started to bring in nest materials. You would be lounging in one of the chairs on the verandah with a book and a drink, half-asleep from the heat, and imagine, or perhaps dream, that something just flew past your ear, and then, awake, you would see the bird fly out again in search of more twigs. The work went on for a week or so and then, after much scrambling and aerial display, the female laid her eggs and began incubating.

I brought a chair over one afternoon while the birds were off feeding and felt the warm little rounded shells and then quickly retreated before the mother returned.

Figaro, Micheline's overweight tabby cat, expressed a passing interest in these two birds and would sometimes lie stretched out under the lamp, but he was too lazy to bother to try to catch one.

By late June the martins had hatched one brood of nestlings and were working on another. The parents were swooping in under the beamed roof at regular intervals with beaks full of insects that they would feed to their young. We could hear their cheeping as soon as the parents would arrive and see their gaping mouths just above the edge of the nest.

Another species of migrant began passing through about this time. A rude couple of pieds-noirs, as the European Algerians were called, booked a room in late June, but they so offended Micheline with their abrupt demands that she became curiously inactive whenever they would ask for something.

"Bring us two *demis*," they would command.

"Straightaway," she would say and rush off to the kitchen behind the bar, where she would sit in a chair just behind the back door of the scullery and smoke a cigarette. After five minutes or so, she would bring out one beer.

"We wanted two," they demanded.

And off she'd go for another five minutes.

Dinners were equally slow, and soon they stopped eating at the restaurant, and then one day, they left.

The same thing happened — unintentionally this time — with two gentlemen from London who were traveling together and checked in, intending to stay for a few days. They were perfectly civilized types who dressed in collared shirts with cravats, stuck to themselves, and were always polite, albeit aloof from the locals.

Staff in the kitchen at the Rose Café had the sometimes unfortunate habit of giving nicknames, such as Herr Komandante, to guests and diners. One evening, one of the visiting Englishmen sent back a plate. Micheline snatched it up and charged into the kitchen, announcing that one of the English *finocchio* was not happy with his dinner. He had followed her in to explain something further, was apparently fluent in both Italian and French, and caught the homosexual reference. Coolly, but still civil, they checked out the next morning.

One night in midsummer a ketch came into the quay and dropped off a strange, silent couple, who arrived at the café and demanded rooms. Micheline went through her usual sham of checking to see if there was space, which there was, and the couple went silently to their room and remained there. They were a handsome pair, both tall and slim with an aristocratic air about them. They had Eastern European accents but French passports.

The couple came down in the morning and ordered coffee and *pain beurré*, and after breakfast they walked to town and did not come back till late in the evening. For three days they followed this routine, rising early, taking coffee and buttered bread, rarely speaking, even to each other. They wore the same clothes every day and did not seem to have much luggage. Then on Sunday night, having collected their papers on fictitious pretenses, they caught the ferry to the continent and left without paying.

While they were there, a Cuban man named Mendoza showed up with his daughter and booked a room for a week. He was of recent Spanish extraction and was cut from the same stone as Vincenzo: dark eyes, high cheekbones, and a mass of curly black hair above a brush mustache. His daughter, Conchita, was a dark-eyed young thing, about fourteen years old. Mendoza was a guitarist who made his living by taking gigs at small local bistros on the Riviera — or so he claimed. In fact, he seemed to have access to private funds; he certainly could not have made very much money at the locales in which he performed. The two of them had been traveling for months, he said. They stayed in Seville, where he still had family; in Malaga; the Balearic Islands; Cannes; and then Nice, where he had played at a local club and where (so he said) he fell in with a rich widow for a few months. He must have retreated to Corsica to untangle himself from some web of love, although he didn't say that.

He and his daughter stayed on for three weeks, and at no charge would sometimes entertain guests on the terrace with Cuban folk tunes and Spanish fandangos. When she was in the mood, Conchita would dance in the flamenco style, snapping her fingers and clapping rhythmically, clicking her tongue and stamping her feet. Chrétien would occasionally attempt to join her when he had had a little too much to drink.

One afternoon about this time I saw a blond man of about forty, with a bulbous nose and little, piggy eyes, sitting on the verandah nursing a beer. I passed his table as I was sweeping the floor, and he asked me if I knew anyplace in the town that rented rooms. I told him we had rooms here, and that he should speak to Micheline.

"Where are you from?" he asked. "Italy?" This was a question that was becoming de rigueur.

I told him and we fell into conversation. He had been hanging around Monte Carlo for a few months, he told me, apparently with some success — until recently.

"Just lost a fortune," he said.

He ordered another beer, which I brought out to him.

"So you're an American, eh?" he stated. "I'll wager you fifty francs you can't name the fifty states."

"No deal," I said. "I can't do it."

I had been around small-time gamblers in Nice long enough
to know that this was an old trick. Very few Americans can
actually name all the states. The petty shills knew it and would
exploit American pride. The blustery patriotic ones would
always take the bet and invariably lose. (Although once, in Nice,
I overheard a well-traveled New York woman take the bet, and
when she started to run out of states begin to make them up —
Texarkana, Ozark, Cayuga. The shill never knew.)

"Look here," the blond man said, "do you know a man in
town named Van Zandt, lives in a big villa somewhere around
Ile Rousse?"

I told him I didn't know such a person, but there was a man
named something like Von Metz who lived outside the town.

"People around here call him le Baron," I said.

"What's he look like?"

"Tall man with white hair, a good dresser."

"That's him. Where does he live?"

I told him he would have to ask the patron, who was at that
hour involved in his midafternoon tryst with Micheline, although
I didn't spell that out for him.

"Go ask the boules players in the town square," I said. "They
all know where he lives, and they'll be down there now; they're
there every afternoon. Are you a friend of his?"

He dodged the question, as I figured he would, but indicated
that he had had some sort of business dealings with the gentleman in the past and would like to pay his respects.

"Sometimes he comes out here late at night to play cards," I
said. "If I see him I'll tell him you were looking for him. What's
your name?"

"Dushko," he said. "What did you say they call him here?"

"Le Baron. I thought his name was Von Metz, though. Might not be the same man."

"No, that's him," Dushko said. "Le Baron, eh?" He laughed privately.

The last of these birds of passage was the man Micheline called Karamazov.

He was a thick-necked man with a wide head and short-cropped black hair, and he was wearing madras Bermuda shorts and a white tennis shirt and sneakers when I first saw him, an unusual costume for that time and place.

"Excuse me," he said in French as I passed his table. "Can one rent a room here?"

"Yes, but I think they're all full," I said. "Come back tomorrow, maybe."

He asked how much we charged, and how much would it be if he stayed for a week or more, would the price be lower, and was there a full pension perhaps, and did I know any similarly isolated spots on this part of the coast where he might spend a week or so?

I noticed that he had an American accent, so I asked him in English where he was from.

"*Les Etats Unis,*" he said.

"Interesting. What state?" I asked.

"*Wisconsin,*" he said, pronouncing the *W* as a *V,* as in French.

"I've been there once," I said. "The Wisconsin Dells. Beautiful. Are you just passing through here?"

"*Non, je travaille ici en France,*" he said.

"You can speak English, if you like, I'm American."

"*Je sais,*" he said.

"*Vous parlez anglais, non?*" I asked.

"*Oui.*"

"I am American, you can speak English with me if you like."

"*Oui, je sais,*" he said.

We chatted on in this way for a while in English and French, with the usual small talk about travels and the weather and the local customs, but I finally asked him why he didn't want to speak English to me. He said he had come to France to learn French and was therefore determined to speak only French, no matter what.

"OK," I said, continuing in English. But I was mystified. He was, after all, a countryman, the first I had talked to in a number of months, and what new French could he possibly learn from me anyway? He was pretty fluent already, although he still had the flat *A* of a Midwesterner.

Micheline gave him a room, and for the next week we would see him around. He was always polite but humorless and, unlike the other guests, not very fun-loving. He would disappear for much of the day and come back for dinner, but somehow Micheline learned that he had studied Russian at Yale in the United States and seemed to know a lot about communism. She was in charge of names in the kitchen and subsequently dubbed him Karamazov. Chrétien picked it up and took to addressing him as "tovarich"—drinking companion—whenever he spotted him at the bar. He would sometimes pound Karamazov on the shoulder and invite him to take a vodka—which of course Karamazov would always refuse. Chrétien's free spirit made him nervous.

The last of the summer sojourners to arrive was Marie. One morning I came up from my morning dip, and there she was on the terrace with her parents, having a café crème and a croissant.

"You're back," I said as I walked by.

She had that contained little angry pout she sometimes assumed when her parents were around.

"Yes, but so is he," she said, glancing back at the dining room. Inside, just selecting his corner table, I could see the old tutor Giancarlo.

Her parents regarded her solicitously.

As the new arrivals began to come in there were also a few departures, some of them poignant.

Eugène, the dentist, left one Sunday on the night ferry. He and I were standing on a little rise behind the kitchen, looking out to the north as the white ferry hove into view. We watched as it slowly materialized out of the green sea, a bright, shimmering, formless thing at first, then something with an apparent struc-ture, and finally, after twenty minutes or so, the details — rounded flared topsides, row upon row of dark ports, upper decks, and pilot house.

Eugène and I had been talking about the life he was about to resume, and at a lull in the conversation, in what must have been for him a brave and intimate statement, he revealed that he spoke a little English.

He stared out at the ferry, started to say something, hesitated, and then decided to make his one and only attempt.

"The big fish comes," he said, smiling proudly.

I didn't bother to correct him.

Mendoza left with Conchita and went around kissing all the women goodbye — first Micheline, then Lucretia, then Maggs, and then a pretty young married woman who had been there for her honeymoon, off and on, since June. The sad part of his departure had come a few nights before though, long after most

of the guests had gone to bed and there remained only the cardplayers, Jean-Pierre and Micheline, and, interestingly enough,
Pierrot, who I think had come out because he was infatuated
with young Conchita. Herr Komandante was still up having a
nightcap, and there was another couple from the village whom I
did not know, a sad-eyed older man and a short, stocky woman
with bobbed hair, too plain to be anyone other than his wife, as
Vincenzo pointed out.

Mendoza had been playing folk tunes and flamenco dances
most of the evening, but as the night wore on he had retreated
to a corner on the verandah to play for himself. No one was paying much attention to the music; they were all lost in their own
dreams or the machinations of the card game. But suddenly in
the midst of the dull silence, Mendoza hit a discordant, ancient
chord, then another, louder, and then he began to sing a *cante
jondo*, the "deep song" of gypsy tradition — slow and sad and all
in a minor key.

Something happened then. The cardplayers put down their
hands and looked over at him as if he had just arrived. What
little conversation there had been at the tables died altogether.
Micheline halted on her way to the kitchen and leaned in the
door frame. Herr Komandante looked up from his drink and
rested his cheek on his right hand.

Mendoza's singing circled the terrace. It snaked into the interior dining room. It moved out across the road and down to
the shore. It flowed out over the harbor and then began to climb
into the hills and ran up into the maquis, sending the goats and
sheep into flight, and then it moved on to the wild mountains,
where nothing endured but the snow and the mouflon. And it
went on and on. He was pouring into his singing something we

had not heard before from him; you seemed to be able to perceive all of history in his tragic minor chants, a lament for the end of time: dark, hopeless, inevitable. The world was immobilized, and when — finally — the singing ended, there was an uncharacteristic, heavy silence. No one applauded, no one breathed, there was only the lap of waters at the shore, the chirrup of a cricket in the rosemary.

For the rest of that evening no one seemed happy anymore. Some dark dream out of the European sleep had been remembered.

chapter nine Herr Komandante

U p until the late 1960s, Corsican society was a structured hierarchy with an old patriarch at the head of the family or clan. Below him there was a related familial pack of male wolves, one or two of whom would be in line to take over the old king's role. Below them were young unmarried men, and then — living side by side in the same households — women.

Wives and mothers held sway within the household and were responsible for provisioning, cooking, serving, cleaning, childbearing, hen-keeping, and tending the dooryard gardens. Within her sphere, the female head of household was the one in control, even though she might have been the one who stood by the kitchen door, spoon in hand, while the males fed and slurped their plonk at a long table. But even beyond the hearth and home, women traditionally maintained a certain amount of power and respect. As with the archetypal character, Colomba, they were often the driving force behind a vendetta, and Corsican women often fought side by side with their men when it came to defense or liberation. During one battle against the French, they poured boiling pitch down onto the struggling soldiers below the walls. There was even a local term for the traditional powerful woman — *tintinajo* — which was also the word for the belled ram that leads a flock of sheep.

Along with mazzeri and signadore, the other group found in varying numbers in the villages of the interior were homosexuals. Ironically, given the strict male mores, they were more or less tolerated, although most overtly gay people would leave the island for the demimonde of Paris or Marseille. But by the 1960s, with the increase in tourism, gay relationships were accepted and were generally met with the classic French laissez-faire, provided the couples did not flaunt themselves publicly. This was especially true in the more cosmopolitan coastal towns and cities, such as Ajaccio, Calvi, and Ile Rousse, all of which had their share of resident continentals.

I had a little glimpse into this world toward the middle of August. I came up from the cove after a swim one afternoon and saw a group of village men huddled around one of the indoor dining-room tables with Jean-Pierre. They were sitting close together, their dark eyes fixed intently on Jean-Pierre, and they were speaking in low, inaudible voices. I couldn't hear a word even though I made excuses to sweep the floors nearby. In due time they rose, and all four of them walked down the terrace steps with Jean-Pierre and stood by a little Deux Chevaux, much battered, with mud and dents from the maquis. They shook hands ceremoniously and departed.

In spite of the apparent weight of the conversation, Jean-Pierre was smiling when he came back up the steps.

Micheline, who had also witnessed the palaver, asked him what it was all about.

"It's Herr Komandante. He was seen with a fifteen-year-old boy at Giulio's. The boy's mother is upset and has called his uncles. So now word is out in the town. They are just telling me the news."

Micheline snickered when she heard the news of Herr Komandante. "Just a question of time, wasn't it?" she said.

"But what can you do?" Jean-Pierre said. He poured himself a pastis and drank a little. "The poor man," he said.

Later that afternoon, I saw a pile of baggage on the terrace. Herr Komandante was sitting inside at the bar with a citron pressé. Jean-Pierre and Micheline were standing next to him, deep in another discussion. Chrétien was behind the bar, making a coffee, eavesdropping.

"What's going on?" I asked when he came back into the kitchen.

"He's leaving," Chrétien said. "He's paid in full for the month, but he's leaving, and he insists on paying the full amount. Jean-Pierre is trying to convince him to stay."

"Good for him," I said. "Poor Komandante."

"What's the difference?" Chrétien said. "The boy is known around town. The uncles just want Herr Komandante to stay away from the village. It's a question of honor on both sides. Herr Komandante, he is ashamed. The villagers know. But they don't want him around, either."

I went out to straighten some of the café chairs and wipe the tables, and watch the talk as I passed to and from the kitchen. Herr Komandante was staring down blankly at the polished-wood bar, elbows spread, his nose buried in his drink. Jean-Pierre was patting his back, talking. The Komandante was nodding his head sadly.

In the end they persuaded him to stay, and at sundown I saw him back at his post on the promontory, his hands deep in the pockets of his striped bathrobe, staring out at the orange sun as it descended into the green sea.

This time I slipped past him without notice.

Herr Komandante was not the same after that. Rather than retreat further into the cover of normalcy that he usually assumed, quarantined as he was at the Rose Café, he became more himself, perhaps freed at last by the obvious indifference and tolerance of Jean-Pierre and Micheline. He became more the sensualist and bon vivant, eating more greedily and drinking heavily, and more overt in his sexual orientation. He stopped going into town, as he normally would do on some evenings, and he took to calling me *hübscher Jungen* — "Pretty Boy." He would eye handsome young men who came to the café with their parents, although he had the good sense to pull this off surreptitiously. He had realized that as long as he was here in the immediate environment of the Rose Café, he was free.

Many who remained here for any length of time found themselves in this position. Perhaps the vista of the pointless little harbor and the town, which were diminished to insignificance by the wide empty sea to the north and the great stacked mountain ridges to the south, gave them perspective.

Late one night, a couple of weeks after his unmasking, I found Herr Komandante quite drunk, alone in the little nook beside the bar. He was singing old sentimental German songs to himself, swinging his glass and toasting people who passed within his view.

"Hey, Pretty Boy," he called out in German when I walked by toward the kitchen. He lifted his glass to me and winked.

"So gehts, nicht wahr? Es ist eine schöne Nacht für Liebe, nein?"

"Sorry?" I said. *"Ich verstehe nicht.* I don't understand."

I knew exactly what he was saying, though.

"On fait ce qu'on peut, je disais. Nicht wahr? What can one do? This is the life," he said.

"I suppose," I said.

"Make a favor, my friend, take a drink with me this night."

I said I would try, and when I was finished with my chores, I poured myself a glass of cold muscat and sat down with him.

He began rambling on in his combination of broken French and English about the darkness back in Germany.

"You are smart young man, maybe? But you don't know Berlin in winter. Weeks on the end," he said. "No sun is there. And so? The sadness." He pretended to weep. "Trouble in the mind, *ja?*" He tapped his forehead with his index finger. "You seek pleasures elsewhere, you see. And then sometimes. Comes the darkness. Even here in Corsica in the light. Sometimes the . . . what you do you call them?" He swirled his hand above his head with a billowing motion.

"Clouds?" I said in English.

"Ja, ja, clouds. *Wolken.* They make you do things. Nicht wahr? Nobody understands the Wolken."

I kept quiet and let him go on. I think Herr Komandante was about forty, which would have made him old enough to have been a soldier. I had always wondered where he was during the war, and I judged that he was drunk enough to talk, so at an opportune moment I asked him outright where he had been during the war years.

"You are knowing the *Hitler Jugend*, perhaps, the Hitler Youth," he said without pause or shame. "Ja, well that was me. But for my part, I am hating Hitler, and not me alone either, you should know — other boys too. But what choice is there? You don't join, they think you are a Jew, so then they just kill you. We are all knowing this. Or in my case worse, maybe the Kaporal finds out that you are homosexual, so, you know . . ." He pressed his palms together in an attitude of prayer and lifted his eyes to the heavens. "You wear the pink badge and the people, they mock you and kick you. Some of those boys went to the camps with the Jews. Kaput. You never see *them* again. I knew fellows like that. A lot of painted boys I knew, did things for money out on the Kurfürstendamm. And do you know the Swings? They are a degenerate group, girls and boys alike, dancing to the American music, long hair, girls painting their nails and sleeping with the boys, all together there, changing bedrooms. Not me. I never wished to be like them, so it was off to the Hitler Jugend for me. Good place to hide. Plus a lot of boys. Sometimes, eh? We used to pleasure ourselves in big groups. The Hitler Youth, not quite so pure as the Führer believed."

He winked.

When he was seventeen he was drafted. He went through a brief training and then was sent out to fight. He said he had no interest whatsoever in fighting; all he wanted to do was to survive. "I was not brave," he confessed.

He lowered his voice at one point. He was sweating in the heat now, smoking sloppily and spilling ashes in his beer.

"Want to know a secret?" he said. "I am telling you something. In the war I am with some soldiers up in Normandy somewhere, we are in a ditch, planning ambush, ja? And along comes a big *troupeau* of the Americans. My gang, we see that we are too few in numbers to fight, and so they all slip back into the woods. Retreat. Not me. I am lying in the ditch, and when the American boys are just a few meters off, I throw out my rifle in the dust and raise my hands: 'Mercy — please.' Of course they take me prisoner. But let me tell you something." He leaned forward. "That's just what I wanted," he whispered. "Not so bad."

The Americans put him in a cellar in a building with a

shattered upper floor, along with some other prisoners. They fed him and gave him dry bedding of straw and hay and kept the group there for a week. Then they herded them into trucks and took them to Le Havre, where he was loaded onto a troop ship.

"Twelve, maybe fourteen days we are on that ship. Rolling around. Some of us sick. And then the trains. We had windows, though. And what beauty we saw. The cities were filthy but then we roll on, a big winding river with a city on the right side of the train, pastures and fields, and fields and green with the horse and the cow, and then big squares of white fences, and then finally, we unload into trucks and come to a big farm with low new buildings, shining in the sun."

They were housed in a newly constructed barracks that smelled of freshly cut pine, with clean latrines and narrow but comfortable cots with rough, clean-smelling sheets. Herr Komandante said that for the first time since the war began, he was comfortable. They ate well, the work was easy — they cut hay, milked cows twice a day, did a little ditching now and then — but they had full breakfasts and big suppers at night with sweating glass pitchers of iced tea and milk. They could write letters, they were supplied with cigarettes, and the guards were lazy. Nobody bothered them as long as they didn't try to run away.

"One day early on there, we are all called out to muster," he said. "Was Sunday, and they have a big midday dinner, then afterward, the boss man, he comes out and gives big speech. We don't know what the hell he is saying, all is English and nobody can understand except one word — 'America.' But he is smiling and spreading his arms. And then we are going out into the barnyard, and there is this big barrel, you see. The guards, all laughing and slapping us on the back. Friendly. Some of us are thinking, *ach*—now it comes, now we are to be killed. But no! They bring out a bag of salt, then ice, then big cream from the dairy. Then sugar, a huge sugar amount. We never see so much sugar. There is a handle, you see, on the barrel, and we share the turning. Maybe half an hour, we turn that handle. Then the guards come with bowls and spoons and they open up the barrel and take out — you know what they take out? Ice cream. Vanilla ice cream! They take big bowls for themselves and go off, then show us — more spoons, more bowls, as much as we want. Everyone is so happy, some of us begin singing the old songs. Some soldiers there, they know harmonies. And the singing goes on into the night. The guards, they are laughing with us. They are just boys like us, you know, narrow-faced American farm boys with bad teeth and straw-colored hair.

"And so every Sunday afternoon it is like that. Ice cream making. Wonderful hot sun. Singing. Every Sunday, this boss with his speeches. 'America,' he says again and again. We understand that but nothing else. But everybody there, they like that boss, they like this prison."

He shook his head and began to laugh bitterly. "That is very funny, nicht wahr? We are all liking this prison."

As far as I could make out, he was somewhere in the Midwest on a big state farm. He said there was a town nearby, and after a few months they were even allowed to go into town, under guard at first, then sometimes on their own. Where would they run to anyway? They didn't know where they were, and by that time not one of them had any loyalty to the Nazi doctrine. It was, Herr Komandante said, the finest place any German man of draft age could spend the war.

He was there for a year.

"Then there comes a sad day for us. Big news in the camp. We are free. War is over. So it's back to Berlin. Back onto the trains, back through the green fields to the dark city. Then the transport ship. There are some horses in that ship, in the hold, I think they are taking them over for food for the refugee camps. And those horses there, they are terrified, they are — what do you say — calling — to be free." He attempted a drunken whinny, throwing back his head. People in the bar looked over. "You can hear them sometimes at night. You know what I am thinking? I am like those horses, I am thinking."

It was late now. Out on the terrace, the card game was breaking up. Chairs were pushed back, Jacquis and André strolled off down the dark causeway toward the winking lights of the town, coats draped over their shoulders. Herr Komandante was slowing down, and finally stopped speaking altogether and just stared at the table in the same way that he had been staring at the bar when Jean-Pierre tried to convince him to stay.

"*Pferd in einer Stall*," he muttered. "Horse in a cage. That's me."

By the time Marie returned, Chrétien had established himself with Karen, the Barefoot Contessa. He rarely discussed with me the intimacies of their relationship, as he had about Marie, which made me think he was getting along quite well. I would see them walking out to the Ile de la Pietra in the afternoons, sometimes alone, sometimes in the company of the Contessa's sister and their annoying young cousin. One afternoon Chrétien and the Contessa did not return until just before the dinner hour, and they were looking flushed and sunburned when they got back. I heard but tried not to listen to a serious, high-speed dressing-down Micheline delivered to Chrétien just before the dinners were served. She had had to set the tables herself and had enlisted me to help, even though I was still cleaning fish for the dinners.

Marie of course noticed all this, and had fallen into an informal détente with Chrétien in which the two of them were civil with each other, even allies of a sort. The fact is, Marie still needed him in her ongoing skirmish with her tutor.

I was headed out to the terrace to have a coffee with Chrétien late one morning, while Marie was trapped in her corner seat with Giancarlo. I saw her beckon Chrétien over silently. Like a loyal dog, he went over and sat down with them. Giancarlo innocently included him in his tedious lecture, and soon Marie excused herself to visit the bathroom. She fled through the back door of the kitchen and headed for the cove.

"Come for a swim," she said to me as she passed.

She was far out on the other side of the cove when I got there, taking her time. I had my fruit basket and went out to collect a few urchins for the midday meal, and once I had a basketful, I joined her on her flat rock.

"So you heard about Herr Komandante," I said.

"Of course. But they should send him back to Berlin. A dirty old German like that. He shouldn't be allowed here. Bothering young boys, it's dirty. He is a disgusting old man."

Marie was not, I had noticed, the most liberal-minded Parisian I had ever met.

We lay there for a while not speaking, allowing the sun to bake us.

Sometimes from that quarter, looking out to the west, the

only thing you could see was the rocky point of the islet with its Genoese watchtower, the blue-green line of the horizon of the ancient Mediterranean, a few passing gulls slipping suddenly over the high rock walls, and nothing more. Had you been somehow mysteriously dropped down into this environment, it would have been hard to identify exactly what era you were living in.

I had been thinking about a conversation I listened in on the day before with Giancarlo and Chrétien: an elaborate, convoluted argument having to do with Henri Bergson's concept of time and the idea that in the human mind, time operates as a continuous flow in which past and present are inseparable from memory and consciousness. Something in that cove, some ineffable sense of the place, the air, and the smell of salt and seaweed and sun on granite had the effect, I noticed, of lifting me out of the present. I was suspended. It seemed to justify Bergson's theory.

I looked over at Marie. She had stripped off her top and was lying on her stomach, with her head turned away, toward the islet, so quiet I thought she might be asleep. I turned over on my side, and telescoped my left hand so as to view the island across her bare back. Her sun-browned shoulder blades and the long sweep of her back, viewed from the proper perspective through my curled fingers, matched almost perfectly the prominence and the flat roll of rocky shoreline on the opposite side of the cove. Even the color was similar, a reddish brown.

"What are you doing there?" Marie murmured, without turning over.

"Oh, nothing," I said in a nasal voice that sounded like Giancarlo's. "I was just thinking about Henri Bergson and how you can't really measure the elements of linear time."

"*Oh mon Dieu que c'est ennuyeux tout ça; tu m'embêtes quelque-fois; vous tous m'embêtez. C'est trop!*"

I laughed. "Sorry," I said.

"Good."

"I apologize."

"OK."

I looked at her for a second, and then without thinking, leaned over and kissed the back of her right shoulder.

"Oh hey, Cowboy, cut that out."

"Sorry."

She groaned in boredom. I think she was trying to sleep.

I was curious to know what Marie intended to do after this summer. She was so indifferent to her studies and didn't seem to have any interests or cares other than dancing and preening like a cat and staying warm. She hated cold. In the brave new world that was forming back in Paris among the students I knew, it was all politics, and Sturm und Drang, and existential angst. People sat in cafés in their black turtlenecks, smoking incessantly and taking on all the problems of the world at large. Marie was more like an American girl in some ways — hazel-eyed and suspended in an indifferent present.

"I forgot you were a Catholic," I said.

"Um," she mumbled.

A gull slipped over the island, white against the azure blue. I watched it disappear over the point of land to the south.

"I say, did you happen to know, by the way of passing, that Henri Bergson believed in direct intuition as a means of attaining knowledge rather than the mechanistic, rational means of scientific, formulaic discovery so commonly employed here in the Western Hemisphere? And did you know, further, that his famous works were banned by the Church?"

She spun over and grabbed me by the throat, pushed me back, and began to strangle me, shaking my head gently against the hot rocks. "You are a crazy cowboy," she said. "Crazy American atheist cowboy. But just the same . . ." Then she kissed me.

"I am going for a swim," she said.

She tracked down through the hot red rocks, waded in, and struck off for the opposite shore with a fast, four-beat crawl.

"Hail Mary full of grace," I called after her in English.

And all the while, Chrétien was getting along famously with Karen. Early one morning, I caught a glimpse of something in white sweep past the stairwell in the upstairs hallway and guessed it was Karen, retreating from a night in Chrétien's narrow little bedroom over the kitchen. Sometimes she joined us in the kitchen peeling potatoes and chopping carrots for Vincenzo. And one afternoon, at a café on a side street away from the square, I saw the two of them nuzzling and kissing at one of the tables.

"She is beautiful, don't you think?" Chrétien asked me.

"Oh yes, in a wild sort of way," I said.

"That's it. A wild animal. But I do not know what kind. Not a gazelle."

Karen had long, loose bangs that fell below her brows, almost covering her eyes.

"An English sheepdog, maybe?"

"A sheepdog?" He thought about it for a minute. "*Non, non.* Not a sheepdog. She's too smart. It's not that — she's too refined."

"A boxer, maybe?"

I tilted my head knowingly toward Nikita, who was asleep (of course — he slept most of the day). He was on his back, paws cocked in the air, mouth open, seemingly dead. I thought he was a profoundly ugly dog.

Chrétien looked back at me without expression. He had an interesting, probably studied, mannerism of not responding to statements that were obviously absurd jokes, as if he didn't get it. Then he would lose control, and after a few snickers break into peals of laughter. Now he snickered, caught himself, and then gave in and let fly with his long, hyena-like laugh and reached across the table and pretended to strangle me.

"I will kill you!" he said in dialect.

chapter ten War and Remembrance

$\dagger$

Back home in the United States, my parents had the unfortunate habit of collecting official-looking mail addressed to me and forwarding it to me in one large envelope. Jean-Pierre handed me one of these dreaded packets one morning, and I began sorting through what seemed to me a pointless collection of extinct bank notices, school fund-raising appeals, and other tedious, inconsequential form letters. But one of these letters had an ominous U.S. Government return address. I opened the envelope and found there an official summons from the draft service. I was to report for a pre-induction physical, the document read — without fail — on April 14. This was now early August, four months past the deadline. I stared dully at the notice for a while, threw it on the table with the other papers, and drank some more coffee. What was I to do?

Out in the harbor, the old *Bagheera* was just making off from the quay. With much backing and filling, the vessel began moving steadily in reverse toward the rocky shore below the café, then swung its bow toward the open waters beyond the jetty and headed out at a slow, steady pace, leaving a faint V-shaped wake astern. She was headed off on her usual rounds of the Mediterranean: Marseille, Toulon, Ceuta, Crete, Naples, Livorno, Bastia, and wherever else she could find a cargo. I had a passing fantasy that I could be on board.

I had been watching this little tramp steamer appear and disappear in the harbor all through the spring and summer. She had no set schedule, and the nature of her cargo was a great mystery to me: a collection of small and large crates, barrels, and boxes, often off-loaded in a pendulous net and dispersed along the quay. Horse-drawn wagons and old motorized trucks, summoned by what mysterious alchemy I did not know, would appear, pick up a selection of crates, and then disappear into the hills and hinterland.

I asked Max one night about the *Bagheera*, but he avoided a direct answer. He merely indicated that she had been coming in and out of the harbor for years — the same thing Pierrot had told me.

"During the war," he said, "she used to carry shipments of arms, ammunition maybe, and radio parts. But these would be deported off the coast, offshore, somewhere else, east of Cap Corse maybe. Nowadays, who knows?"

He knew, of course. But I waited.

Then I dared to ask if any of the cargo that was off-loaded went up to the Baron's.

"Le Baron's?" he said, surprised. "No, why do you ask?"

"I don't know. There are stories."

"About what?"

"His money. How he gets his money. Somebody told me he was a smuggler."

Max laughed. "That's what everyone says. If somebody out here has money, he must be contrabandist."

"Is he?"

Max laughed again, a forced laugh this time. "Maybe. Probably no. In fact definitely no. I think."

"So how did he get so rich? And why does he live out there on the edge of the maquis in solitude?"

"I thought you knew," Max said.

I told him what I had heard from Fabrizio.

"And you believed that?"

"I don't know, Vincenzo said Fabrizio is a crazy old liar. A mazzeru, even."

"Maybe," said Max. "Maybe no. Part true, maybe. But I know le Baron, he was in Nice during the war, and he was somehow attached to Vichy. But then, you know, the espionage is the espionage. He was reverse spy, it could be. Anything was possible back then. He does not seem the Vichy type."

He began to spill out various permutations of unoccupied France. Max said he thought the Vichy thing might have been a cover and that le Baron was connected to the anticommunist White Russian community in Nice, and that he was a Gaullist but at the same time was helping to undermine the communist cell of the resistance around Nice. He snatched arms shipments intended for the communists and then turned the arms over to the Gaullist resistance fighters and even tipped off the Milice, the local Vichy police thugs, as to the whereabouts of certain communist leaders.

"Was dog eat the dog over there, you know. Here not so bad. Everyone here in Corsica, we all hate the Nazi — the bandit, the mothers, the childrens, the bankers. We all hate the fascists. The mountain people up in the villages, if the Boches come looking for you, and you can mount into the hills, in the little villages, the peasants, they put you in the barn, bury you in the hay. Then when the Nazis come, they look them in the eyes and sign themselves" — Max crossed himself — "and they say, oh yes, they saw you headed for Bastia, over the mountains. They show the trail you took. Later, maybe that night. Boum. Boum. One less Nazi. But over on the continent, big dog fight. Communist,

Gaullist, and local criminals, still arguing among each others. But all want to kill first the big dog, the Nazi, so they can get on top, you see."

"What about that weird yacht with the wishbone rig that comes in at night and always leaves before dawn?" I asked.

"That's from Nice. We see it come, we see it go. One knows nothing. One does not ask. But probably this is a friend of le Baron."

"And the *Bagheera* — what do you think it carries now?"

"Who knows? That's not my trade. Not my business. She carries what must be carried."

"Kif, maybe?"

He looked at me and raised an eyebrow. It was apparently a good guess.

"Why you say this?"

"Just a guess."

"No. No kif."

"Hashish?"

Max drew a breath and sighed. He was getting tired of this.

"Who knows. I am sixty years, you know. I have seen the wars. Who knows what *le Bagheera* carries — kif, hashish, guns, cigarette, whiskey, women — who cares. It is not our business. In Ajaccio, one sees the big bandit, the capu, the vendetta. Up in the mountains, the country men come to town — to Mass even — with guns slung over their shoulders. I am tired of all this, you see. These little ants. You kick over their hill and they swarm out. Just don't kick the hill, eh? Allow me to give you a little lesson of life."

"What's that?"

"Don't worry about things."

A few nights after the draft notice arrived, Chrétien and Gian-carlo had a heated discussion that started with André Gide's idea of the *acte gratuit*, the pointless, motiveless crime that sums up the meaningless existential universe and serves only to establish the fact that one is truly free. That led to a discussion of the theoretical morality of killing someone — in this case Hitler. Giancarlo argued that the murder of Hitler would be the oppo-site of the gratuitous crime committed by Lafcadio in Gide's *Les Caves du Vatican*, and would have been an ethical, preordained act that — sixth commandment notwithstanding — would even assure the killer entrance into the Christian heaven, "...were such a place to exist," he added.

The argument became more and more heated and expanded into the morality of war in general and ended up, as these talks often would do, with the Second World War, which, as Chré-tien argued (for the sake of argument alone, it should be said; he was a pacifist), was the only ethical war he could think of. This discussion was taking place indoors, near the bar, and the hedonists who had gathered around the bar that night, includ-ing Herr Komandante, were getting nervous and moving away, as if to shun any mention of the war would cause the memory of it to disappear.

I had just read *Les Caves du Vatican* as part of a French civi-lization course at the Sorbonne and was inclined to join the discussion. Not only that, the draft notice had gotten me worried that I would, at some point, have to make a commitment — an existential act, as my friends back in Paris would argue — that would be a statement of the way that I would have the universe function. I wasn't buying it, though. I was more in the camp of Marie and Herr Komandante.

In the past, when it came to commitment to violence or war, the Corsicans did not seem to have a problem. The only debate on the subject that I know of occurs in the case of Mérimée's character, Orso della Rebbia, who had been influenced by continental mores.

When Orso waffles as to avenging his father, Colomba outlines the chain of absolute necessity that requires Orso to act. For one thing, everyone in his native village of Pietranera expects him to carry out the vendetta. It is his duty as his father's son. He wavers, finds excuses not to seek revenge. He accepts the cover-ups that had protected his father's murderer and summons memories of his civilized comrades in the drawing rooms of Paris and the English lady who has promised to be his bride. But Colomba presses in.

Traditionally in Corsica, the women would carry the blood-soaked shirt of a victim of a vendetta. Colomba hands Orso a little chest at one point that contains the bloody shirt his father had been wearing when he was killed, and she places the two rusted bullets that took his life on the shirt. Then she leaves Orso alone, hoping that the terrible relics will exert the inherent spiritual force that will force him to act. She seems to have retreated to the ancient pagan belief, not uncommon on Corsica, that the actual blood of a murdered relation literally cries out for vengeance.

The barricaded tower of Orso's ancestral enemy, the family Barricini, is just across the square, and here the murderer lies secluded, an aged and doddering man now, protected by two violent sons, hot to kill. Orso finally decides to take his revenge on these two country toughs rather than the father, who actually carried out the murder. But even then he refuses to kill them outright, and instead challenges them to a fair duel. Later, on a narrow road between two stone walls, the two brothers ambush Orso and wound his arm. Nonetheless he manages to get off two quick shots, and when the smoke clears, he finds that he has killed the two brothers.

Mérimée points out in a footnote that this fictional account is based on actual events that took place while he was staying in one of the isolated mountain villages on Corsica.

What was true for local revenge killing was true also in the larger sense. Over the three-thousand-year period of invasion, whenever Corsicans were not happy with the current political regime, they would take to the hills and carry on their ancient custom of resistance. This was no less true when the Romans and the Genoese invaded than it was when the fascists moved in.

In 1943, shortly after the German and Italian invasion of Corsica, the Allied forces contacted the maquisards and began to arrange clandestine supply drops, some of which were carried out in daring landings at obscure beaches along the east coast. The *Casabianca*, one of twelve French submarines that were docked in Toulon in November of 1942 when the Germans took over, was one of the heroes of this period. All the other submarines in the port were sunk by the British in order to keep them from falling into German hands, but the *Casabianca* escaped and joined the Allied naval forces in North Africa.

Under the command of Captain Jean L'Herminier, the vessel began making daring arms drops on the coasts, hiding by day on the sea bottom like a moray eel, and then approaching the beaches under cover of darkness to off-load its cargo. In September 1943, the Italians abandoned their alliance with the Germans. Later that month, the *Casabianca* dropped off 109

Free French shock troops, who joined the local maquisards. By October, after some severe fighting with the Germans around Nebbiu and Bastia, the resistance finally drove the Nazis out. It was the first section of France to be liberated.

Thinking all this over, it struck me later that there was a certain irony that I should find refuge from military service in the heart of one of the most violent corners of Europe.

We had another bout with the libeccio at this time. It began, as it often did, in the late afternoon, and although it subsided a little at dusk, it came back with another driving blast around midnight. I could hear it hammering the shutters up in the main building, working over the waves in the cove, and howling through the rocks. It was still blowing the next day, the flags and pennants on the yachts in the harbor standing out straight and the halyards slapping incessantly. We waited for dusk, and watched as it subsided around sundown. We had dinner and listened with disappointment as it came up again later in the evening. Dawn the next day was a bright red line of fire, but you could see huge flocks of sheep (the French term for whitecaps) grazing all across the bright blue Mediterranean, all the way out to the horizon. The wind was nonstop, hour on hour of blasting buffets, all through the following night, a white moon illuminating the waters beyond the cove, the silvery white sheep winking in the open sea against the black waters. And it was there again at dawn, pounding, the surf now rising against the causeway, the libeccio catching the spray and sending it in flying sheets over the road to the little beach on the east side. At the end of the cove it was even worse. My cottage was perched high in the rocks and was safe, but the waves began breaking over the causeway that carried on to Ile de la Pietra. No one came out that third night. The guests huddled in the inner dining room, drank cognac and coffee, and sat around in small groups talking, more social than usual, trapped indoors by their common enemy, the wind.

That night something awakened me. Something was different. I could hear the sea surge, the grate of spray on the roadway, the growl of rocks, and the shudder of breaking waves. But the relentless howling had ended. The beast had died.

I lit a candle and went outside. The kindly, moist, warm air had returned and was laden with salt and flowers and the dank scent of moss and algae. I went up to the promontory and sat down on one of the rocks, watching the sheeplike waves sparkling in the moonlight.

This was, after all, I was thinking, a benign corner of the earth: a few nasty winds, a spell of cold in winter, too much heat for a few weeks in summer, but basically a green refuge against the dark events that clashed across the continents beyond.

Lost in this benevolent reverie, I heard someone behind me and turned to see Maggs. She hadn't seen me and had climbed to one of the higher rocks and was standing there, holding her white terry-cloth robe at her throat.

"Oh, you too?" she said, spotting me.

She came down from the height and sat next to me. "What are you doing up so late? Couldn't sleep?"

I told her I would sometimes wake up in the wind, get an idea, and light the candle, but tonight it had been the lack of wind, the strange stillness.

She was not looking her best, I noticed, even in the pale light of the moon. Sleep — or maybe tears — had puffed up her eyes; she looked tired in the shadows, somewhat haggard. She leaned forward on her propped knees, yawned periodically, and shook back her hair, running her hand back along the side of her head nervously. I couldn't help noticing, when her robe fell open at one point, that she was unclothed beneath. But this was no situation for intimacies, she was distracted.

"Bad dream?" I asked.

"Yes," she said, yawning again. "The usual."

She looked over and saw my notebook.

"What do you do, wake up and write?"

"Yes, if I can't sleep. But it's not a good thing to do. It keeps me awake."

"I should write. Maybe that would evict my dreams," she said.

I didn't dare ask her what her dreams were about, but she began to tell me anyway, something about a rain of fire. The stage for this drama was always the Warsaw Uprising, she said.

"There are people who were there who say it was something so horrible that it is impossible to speak about and impossible to keep quiet about. I don't know which is better," she said.

Her family had had money, she explained, and had lived out in the country beyond the city, in a villa with some land. They had been evicted and relocated in the city. I had heard some of this story already, but never the details.

"For us, it wasn't so bad, really. We had a big enough flat on Marszalkowska Boulevard — my two younger brothers, father, mother, and Aunt Wanda, who lived with us. Uncles and their families coming up for dinner sometimes on Sundays. We had enough food. My father had some sort of connections and we had enough food, even wine sometimes with meals, and schnapps and vodka. It wasn't the way it used to be out in the country where we lived. But I made some friends. I even knew that officer from the German Army. We would talk. He was smart, and I think he too came from money."

She knew perfectly well there were hideous atrocities going on in the Warsaw Ghetto: "Who couldn't know?" she said. And there were periodic bombings and skirmishes in the streets between the partisans and the occupiers, and of course there was the Ghetto Uprising itself, in 1943. But all that had been contained, more or less separated from her world. Then it all changed after 1944, after the Warsaw Uprising.

The familiar world was turned upside down. The days didn't differ from one to another in that season in hell, she said.

"Howls of bombs, airplanes, roarings in the sky, and our building, it just shook like a rat in the jaws of a terrier one night. Our whole building. Windows crashing, clattering all around, and out in the streets, the smoke and fires — smoke first, then the little tongues of flames, and then whole walls of flame. What a terrible night that was, people running everywhere, dead animals, and Aunt Wanda moaning: 'Oh my God,' she says. 'Oh my God, Sacred Heart of Christ,' she says, 'oh my God.' Even back then, I am thinking, what does God have to do with all this? This is hell itself.

"But then it stopped, and we went outside and walked around in the dark ashes and the smoke, and while we're out there, comes another howling, like evil bats or predatory birds, and then the thuds all around the city. You hear the noise, first the roaring, then the whining, then the *thud* and the explosions. I don't know, in some ways I was angry with the partisans. Why didn't they just leave it all alone, the Jews in their ghettos, the Nazis in our streets? Nazis in our best restaurants, why not just carry on? And just then, low over the building, a big bomber roars over. It was huge and all dark with widespread wings; it was evil incarnate, and then I was thinking, my God, what can you do but fight that. The brave partisans, just kids really. Your age. We lost. German tanks everywhere finishing things off, great smoldering piles where apartment buildings once stood, courtyards where children once played, courtyards, windows, doors, twisted pipes, all in a heap. One building I saw had a bathtub hanging from a standing wall by its pipes, as if it too had been executed, like all the other partisans. The whole city in ruins with people picking through the rubble, looking for potatoes, for coal bits, for evidence of loved ones, maybe. They lost, the partisans. The city lost. Hitler wanted to make an example of Warsaw. Maybe two hundred thousand people dead, no place to sleep for the living, no food.

"We were all in a shelter one night, I remember, my family and I, and someone came in and said they had hit Sisters of the Sacrament."

She blew out her breath and laughed cynically.

"What an irony, that. Those were the nuns who had voluntarily sealed themselves up against the world. Young women, they would go in there, away from the temporal world, behind grated doors and windows, away from secular life altogether. They thought they could find peace. You go in, take the vows, and you never come out. You're safe. They sang hymns to God and chorales, they held communions, they prayed, they dressed in white and lived a spiritual life, waiting for ascension or salvation from sin or whatever it is they believed in. They were fools, weren't they? Along come the German shells and lay bare their sanctuary; the walls collapse, the interior is revealed, and we see dead nuns in the rubble, still in their virginal whites.

"You see what I mean? Nothing saved. Nothing sacred. Nothing untouched by that deadly rain, and don't think I am the only one who dreams of a rain of fire, anybody who was there must have the same repetitive dream; they just don't talk about it."

She looked off at the sea. All across the black waters, the white breakers were winking on and off.

"I was only eighteen when it rained . . ." she said. Her voice cracked.

I couldn't say anything. The light had faded. The joy in the clink of ice in a summer glass. A flight of sparrows. Her curiosity.

After a few minutes' silence I said that I had better go back to bed, on the excuse that I always had to get up early to make Pierrot's coffee.

"Yes, that's excellent. Make his coffee for him tomorrow morning. That sounds so good. Maybe I'll join you. It's all right. I'm sorry," she said. "It was the wrong time."

"Will you be all right?" I asked.

"Of course. Awake, out here, with the scrambling sea. What can possibly go wrong? It's sleep that's dangerous," she said.

chapter eleven ## Le Baron According to André

J ean-Pierre came in from the market with a load of local, grass-fed beef a few days after the libeccio dropped, and Vincenzo set to preparing it for a local dish of veal with wild mushrooms — not a typical item on the Rose Café menu. He braised the veal in eau-de-vie and olive oil, then cooked up a few slices of onion and garlic, put back the veal with a few crushed tomatoes, and sautéed it a little more, whereupon he dumped in white wine, another dash of eau-de-vie, and a handful of herbs from the maquis, and then let the whole thing stew. Later he sautéed the mushrooms and stirred them in.

The pot was sitting there on the stove, and as I passed I couldn't help dipping in a hunk of bread to taste it, a trick I had learned from the cardplayers, who would always come sniffing around in the kitchen tasting the dishes if they happened to arrive early.

The sauce had that heady flavor of the wild forest.

I noticed that André had been coming out earlier and earlier during those weeks, and I would often see him at the bar with Peter and Maggs and Herr Komandante, chatting in that odd polyglot combination of languages that the international guests at the Rose Café seemed to be able to assume whenever they wanted to socialize. The man who called himself Dushko happened to be there that night, although he was staying someplace else back in the town.

Of all the periodic visitors at the café, Dushko was the most linguistically versatile; he spoke most of the Romance languages, as well as German and a couple of Slavic languages, and even, I was told by another guest, Hungarian — an impossible language with no apparent relatives in Europe other than a vague association with Finnish and Estonian.

Conversation at the bar was lively but required a little help with translation for André, who spoke only French and the local patois, plus a little Italian. I noticed that Maggs, who was fluent in French, as well as Russian, German, and Polish, was acting as his translator. And I also noticed that she seemed to be filling out the intent of the conversation and the innuendos, as well as the literal words, and that André seemed surprisingly interested in what was being said, so much so that he managed to draw her away into a conversation of their own.

Peter, who was ever the stiff-upper-lipped Englishman, also spoke French and remained above it all, commenting politely and laughing at the appropriate moments. At one point, when the conversation turned to fish, he joined in. He was an avid spear fisherman. In fact that's about all he did, unless the wind was up. On those days he read in the corner of the dining room, nursing a pot of tea.

They were all chatting there happily when le Baron came in. He greeted everyone, ordered a drink, and at one point in the chatter, asked me to tell Jean-Pierre that he would be having dinner that night with Dushko, whereupon the two of them ordered another round and retreated to a table far out on the terrace.

"Who is that guy?" André asked Maggs, as Dushko left.

"I don't know, but he speaks Polish," she said. "I can't place his accent, though. German I think."

"But he has an accent in German, too," Herr Komandante said.

"And in French," André added.

"He's probably Czech or Hungarian," Peter suggested. "One of those blokes who gets uprooted, flees his country, drifts around Europe picking up languages, working for whoever will pay, and then can't figure out where he belongs after the war."

They all stared out at the terrace where le Baron and Dushko were now seated.

"Cards tonight, André?" Maggs asked, indifferently.

"But of course. Cards every night."

"Don't you chaps have anything else to do?" Peter asked.

The tone, as far as I could determine, was neutral. But André glanced at him before answering, fixing him with a mean squint.

"We are all friends," he said. "Friends play cards."

They turned their attention to the terrace again.

Dushko was leaning across the table toward le Baron, speaking with animation, cupping his fingers upward in the southern Italian style, flailing his left hand in the air. Le Baron was smoking lazily, eyeing Dushko through the smoke.

"What do you think it's all about?" I asked from the other side of the bar.

"Money," André answered without pause and without turning from the scene on the terrace. "He's probably trying to float a loan."

"How do you know that?" Maggs asked.

"I know le Baron," André said.

"Where is le Baron from?" Peter asked in all innocence. "I thought I heard an accent in French."

"He says he's Belgian, but who knows?" André said. "Could be German, too. Alsatian maybe. Von Metz, or whatever his name is. He's just another con artist. On the lam, found a good place to hide."

No one was overly interested in this definitive bit of news but me. They went back to their small talk. André engaged Maggs. Peter ordered another beer; Herr Komandante sipped his muscat and watched the incoming dinner guests.

"Does le Baron speak German?" I asked Herr Komandante.

"I don't think so — not to me, anyway," he said. "But who knows?"

In due time Maggs and Peter departed for their table, leaving André and the Komandante. Karen and her troupe arrived and engaged Herr Komandante, who, I noticed, seemed to have an eye for young Laurent.

"You think le Baron is a swindler?" I managed to ask André. "You sure?"

"But of course. Big-time smuggler and forger. You didn't know? He was a double agent during the war. He was connected to the communists and the bandit gangs up in the Dordogne. Soleil and that crowd, you know, political but criminal at the same time."

Soleil, I learned, was a criminal turned resistance fighter from the Marseille area. He was just one of any number of underworld figures, many of them Corsican, who had joined the legitimate resistance fighters and used their art to aid the cause. The Free French and the British were not opposed to cooperating.

"He could also have been working with the Gaullist network," André added. "He was educated in London, speaks good English, and used to arrange shipments from the British SOE, the

Security Office; they trusted him. But then he would manage to allow the criminal gangs to get to the air drops first. That's where he learned his trade. Then he started selling arms to whoever would pay. And then after the war ..."

André waved his hand, indicating that after the war le Baron simply carried on his trade.

"He first came out here during the war to hide out. Things must have gotten hot for him on the continent, and maybe the British were after him as well as the Germans. He was up in the maquis somewhere, and he liked it here. So after the war he comes back with a younger woman and buys that big villa out there. She's a recluse, spends all her time in the garden. I don't think anyone has ever even seen her. Except maybe Jean-Pierre."

I looked back at the terrace. Le Baron and Dushko were sharing a big, high-piled bowl of urchins, stripping out the meat with narrow little forks and tearing off hunks of bread. They ate slowly, and were sharing a cold bottle of local white. Whatever subject had so animated Dushko seemed to have been resolved.

chapter twelve The Artful Dodger

I had heard from Pierrot that somewhere up behind the village of Speloncata, where there were some interesting grottoes, there were thought to be some menhirs and torri. His directions were vague, and he wasn't even sure they were located near Speloncata, but on one of those hot days when a sojourn in the mountains is refreshing, I took off.

As the summer wore on, I managed to negotiate free days for myself by arranging — with Chrétien's help — to have Karen take over my position one day a week as dishwasher. I would often take advantage of these times and go off by myself into the hills. Pierrot would give me a ride on his *moto* to the edge of town, and I would either walk or sometimes hitchhike higher and higher into the mountain slopes beyond the maquis, and then return before dusk, in time for dinner.

On this particular day, I hitched a ride on the back of a truck that dropped me in the hills somewhere south of Ile Rousse and began a long, more or less pointless walk, following donkey trails now and then in those sections that vaguely resembled the descriptions Pierrot had given me. In one village, Pioggiola, I stopped at the one café there and had a coffee and asked about the monuments. No one knew anything about them, but they suggested the next village. So I hiked on.

The roads became more and more rutted and the villages, such as they were, more and more run-down — some were mere piles of stones, half in ruins and inhabited, it seemed to me, only by old people and middle-aged women with gaunt faces and scraggly hairdos. In one collection of houses, a crone with a W-shaped mouth was sitting in a chair in the sun, and as I walked by she uttered a long, incomprehensible sentence in dialect and then cackled maliciously and shook her finger at me. I stopped and asked her in Italian — the closest language I had to the local dialect — if she knew about any stoneworks in the area. She pointed at me, continued to shake her finger in warning, and strewed out a long unintelligible answer. I thought I caught just one word: *morte*, "death," and I couldn't help but wonder if she was a mazzera and was warning me not to continue.

Nevertheless, I waved and hiked on. I was clearly a long way from the cosmopolitan terrace of the Rose Café and the busy town square at Ile Rousse.

The old woman was not out of place here, and in fact was mild compared with some of the other characters that appear in Corsican history and legend. Homer had identified half-wild, man-eating giants on Corsica. Seneca, who was banished to the island in AD 41, portrayed the place as a barren, rocky wasteland — without sustenance. Balzac, who was stranded in Ajaccio at one point, praised the beauty of the island — as did the ancient Greek merchant sailors — but Balzac felt the interior was inhabited by a somber, paranoid race that isolated itself in a mountain fastness. Flaubert passed through Corsica the same year as Mérimée and, like Mérimée, enjoyed the lawless freedom of the people of the maquis, although he perhaps tended to place them in the same romanticized category as Rousseau's natural man. Alexandre Dumas, author of *The Corsican Brothers*, also overemphasized the romance of the place.

In fact, life on Corsica was never easy: The land is not suited to agriculture because of the mountainous terrain; sustenance was hard-won; and, as in isolated cultures the world around, the local people tended to be withdrawn and suspicious of snooping foreigners. Nevertheless, from the perspective of an outsider, the island does have a flair of the exotic — the nearest of the far-flung places, as the English used to claim: great green peaks rising above the scented foothills, misty chasms, waterfalls and rushing streams, rocky sea coves and isolated sandy beaches; and handsome, dark-eyed men in black corduroy and bright red sashes, women in flowing dark skirts and the traditional *messera*, a long, flowing mantilla. And also danger. Armed men, even at church, and powerful, possibly treacherous women (Colomba carried a stiletto inside her messera). Mérimée managed to evoke all this and at the same time portray the tough realities of life in the interior.

All this is not to say that Corsicans themselves did not have a local poetic tradition. There were a few urban writers who attempted to portray the island life, but they were perhaps too close to their world to give an accurate perspective. There was also a regional tradition of improvised verse performed by a *voceratrice*, a woman who invented rhymed laments over a body at a ritual wake. These imaginative verses can go on at length, and they were still being practiced when I was there. One of the last *voceratrice* was interviewed in the mid-1960s by the best of the modern-day interpreters of Corsican life, Dorothy Carrington, for her seminal book *Corsica: Portrait of a Granite Island*. Carrington's *voceratrice* explained that it was not she herself who was singing, but that the voices came to her from the other side.

Beyond the last village on a spur road, the track gave out altogether, and I began following a sheep trail that ran up into the hard foothills. After an hour or so of hiking, skirting all the while a great, granite, east-facing escarpment, I came upon evidence of another dying island tradition, a stone hovel, rounded, with a corbelled roof. From a distance I thought this could have been the ruins of a torri, but when I drew closer, I could see that this pile of stones was actually a shepherd's summer quarters. There was bedding inside, and there was a well-used cooking ring of stone nearby.

Transhumance herding was still going on in the mountains in Corsica at this time. Each winter the shepherds would graze their flocks in the lowlands near the coast, where the pastures were green and snow-free. As soon as the snows melted back from the high pastures, they would bring the flocks up, a journey that could take as much as a week or two. The sheep would spend the summer feeding on the fresh, snow-fed grasses in the high meadows, and then, with the first frosts, start to move down to the coast again.

Earlier in the spring, when I first came out to the island with Armand and Inge, we had taken a bus from Calvi up to a little town in the central mountains called Calacuccia. A few days later we hitched a ride to Ajaccio in the bed of a truck, and on the way down we were halted en route by an immense sea of baa-ing sheep, headed up to the summer pastures.

They were led by a ram with a bronze bell, and there were four or five dogs busily keeping the sheep together as they moved upward. Behind the dogs was a shepherd with a staff, and there were two other men on either side of the flock. In back of them were two donkeys, overloaded with baggage, and behind that there was a wagon pulled by an old nag with a white nose and suspicious eyes.

The men were a rough-looking bunch — unshaven, dressed in many layers of ragged clothing and double-breasted suit jackets, much worn at the elbows — and although one or two of them greeted the driver of the truck, for the most part they kept their eyes on the flock and passed without so much as a word. The man in the wagon was more friendly. He wore the traditional black corduroy, and when he spotted the lovely Inge he whistled and lifted his hat as he passed, and clucked as if to say sorry, but this is the old way, this is the way it's done, and that infernal machine of a truck will just have to wait for the sheep. Inge waved at him with both hands, fluttering her fingers.

I had carried with me into the hills a big tranche of Pierrot's bread, a hunk of sheep cheese, and half a bottle of a local white wine from Cap Corse, and I settled with my back to the wall and had some lunch. Then I stretched out after eating and was soon asleep — daily naps were a part of everyone's routine at the Rose Café.

In my sleep, I was vaguely conscious of the sound of running water and sheep bells in the distance, and when I woke, I followed the sound of the water and came to a small, bounding stream. I washed my face, drank some of the clear water, and was headed back to pick up my pack when I saw an old man with a dog making his way along the escarpment, followed by two or three belled goats. We met at the tiny stone hovel.

He was a wiry old type, cut in the same style as Fabrizio — dressed in a corduroy suit and a dirty flannel shirt, buttoned at the neck. He wore a cloth cap and a cartridge belt, and slung over his shoulder was a long-barreled rifle. He also had a mean-looking dagger stuck inside his cummerbund.

In spite of his fierce demeanor I did not fear for my safety when he first appeared. I had not heard of any kidnappings here on the island, and I knew also that one of the old traditions of the vendetta culture of Corsica was that strangers were out of bounds. In any case, this man was no bandit; he had kindly old eyes and smiled as he approached.

He greeted me in dialect, and when I returned the greeting in French he switched languages, but his French was so accented, or so mixed with dialect, that I could hardly understand him. I was far from the coast at this point, several miles above Fabrizio's compound and in a relatively remote area, so I was not surprised by his broken French. I tried Italian, he went back into dialect, and together we managed to communicate — a little.

All I could understand was that he and his dog were searching for a lost goat. I did catch a few other phrases, *alla campagna*, for example, which was a local term for an outlaw, or someone who makes his living in the hills illegally. I think I also heard him say something about people who live in Bastia. The name *Bastiaccio* here in the interior was a derogatory term. Mountain people distrusted the *Bastiese*, I had heard. They were a race apart and not dependable. (Of course the Bastiese said the same thing about the mountain people — a somber, cheerless race.) I gathered that what the old man was telling me was that someone had stolen his goat. Probably a Bastiaccio.

I offered him a little wine, which he accepted and drank in the Spanish style, holding the bottle above his open mouth and swallowing without closing his lips. Then I asked him about the little stone cabine. It was not his apparently, but was used by a shepherd who passed through this valley in summer. He told me a long story following this which was totally lost on me, although I feigned comprehension, agreeing and nodding with interest. I think it had to do with the shepherd who lived in the cabine and I think he was saying that he was not coming back this year.

"*Bene*," he said, after a few minutes. "*Vadu cercare di piu questu maldettu chevre*" — I'm going to search for that cursed goat, and he tipped his hat and wandered off. I watched him descend toward the stream and disappear into the thickets of holm oak and beech, the goats and the dog tagging along. He was a sprightly old man, a little like a goat himself.

On a hunch, I calculated that if I followed the stream downhill, bushwhacking, I would come to the road I had left earlier in the day, so I followed him and then turned downhill through a relatively open stony forest. A few hundred yards downstream, I could see another clearing off to my right, so I went over to investigate, still half-hoping to find a torri, and came to another pasture, where I picked up a sheep trail back to the road.

The intermittent vistas from this height were spectacular. I could see a whole descending range of maquis and flat pasturelands falling toward the distant blue sea. Behind me there loomed a vast, ominous peak, Monte Pardu, I think, clothed on the lower slopes with a local species of evergreen known as laricio pine. The air was cool; the sun was warm; the rising mixed odor of maquis and forest filled my lungs; and I swung along the open road, refreshed and free and young, with no baggage of any sort weighing me down and no thoughts other than those of the moment. I could hear the cry of rooks, the sound of rushing streams, and the throaty jangle of cowbells from the unseen high pastures, and presuming myself alone, I began a skipping jig and started to sing aloud as I tripped onward and downward toward the sea and whatever future awaited me beyond these sceptered shores.

I got back into town in the late afternoon and stopped at a café at the north end of the plaza, away from the boule pitch and my usual haunt. I ordered a beer and sat stretching my legs, watching the little children wheel round and round on the pointless carousel. Daydreaming there, I heard a familiar French-inflected English greeting behind me. It was le Baron himself, dressed in his linen suit and carrying his leather wallet.

"What are you doing down here?" he asked. "Shouldn't you be cleaning fish?" He was joking, of course, but I explained, even though he probably already knew, that I was taking days off.

"Mind if I join you?" he asked.

I nodded and waved my hand toward the free chair. He ordered a local beer, and we sat talking about the Rose Café and some of the guests and the poor lonely dentist, Eugène, and the outing of Herr Komandante. This eventually brought him around to Marie.

"She's a devilish little scamp, isn't she? Flirting with poor Eugène and all the others. Throwing over Chrétien as she did."

"He saw it coming," I said. "I was with him the day Karen and her sister arrived. He was taken from the start."

"No need to worry about Chrétien, I suppose."

"No, he can take care of himself."

"I say, how well do you know Marie?" le Baron asked.

"Pretty well. We talk. She thinks I'm a cowboy. She likes to hear about American life."

"I think there's more to it than that," he said.

"Maybe."

He drank, looked over at the bank.

"*Tu parla italiano?*" he asked, seemingly out of nowhere.

"*Si un po, perché?*" I answered.

"That's what I thought," he said. "How about Spanish?"

"Yes, I lived there before I came to France."

"German?"

"No. A little. But why do you ask?"

"We see you shuffling around like a peasant from the maquis — limited French, pretending to be Italian around English speakers. Your friend Maggs was telling me she thinks it's your trick, right? Makes it easier to eavesdrop, doesn't it?"

"Not really, I like languages. I just listen. I don't speak any one language very well, though."

"Right, I saw you eavesdropping on that Dushko fellow. He knows a lot of languages."

"I noticed," I said. "Where's he from anyway?"

"Dushko, ah, Dushko," he said with sad resignation. "Who knows where Dushko is from. That's probably not even his name."

"He was looking for you when he first came out here," I said. "I'm afraid I tipped him off. I hope that was OK."

"Sure, he would have found me anyway. And it doesn't matter."

"Who is he?"

He laughed. "Who is Dushko? Now there's a good question. Just don't ask Dushko. He doesn't know who he is. He's a gambling man. A man without a country, blown across borders by the winds of war. He's got any number of personae. Take your pick."

"Peter thought that. Buffeted around by wars?"

"To say the least," he said into his beer.

Dushko, he explained, was one of those entrepreneurial types who seemed to be able to get himself out of any scrapes he fell into. Le Baron said he thought Dushko might be a Czech Jew or maybe a Serb, and had managed to survive the war a free man — mostly. He had been in business in Berlin before the war, he said, and was associated with some left-wing group that was opposed to the rising tide of fascism. He had a lot of connections in the international community, and he and a compatriot got the idea of running arms into Spain during the Civil War. He had contacts everywhere by then and wasn't afraid to use them. At first he sold arms to the Republicans, but he got caught and thrown in prison. Then he cut some deal, got himself free, switched camps, and started selling guns to the Falangists. But he still had his old Republican contacts, le Baron said, and may still have been working with them. After the war, he escaped through Perpignan and disappeared into the refugee camps with the other Republican Spaniards. When the Second World War broke out, someone — probably in revenge — turned him over to the Gestapo for some unidentified crime and he ended up in prison again, back in Germany, in Berlin.

"I think he got knocked around a bit while he was there. Somebody didn't like his attitude. Or maybe they thought he had information," le Baron said. "He was in solitary confinement but, you know — he made contacts — communication by tapping on pipes, that sort of thing."

Le Baron said that somehow, Dushko bartered his way out and after that ended up in Istanbul. He had no country by this time, no allegiances to anyone, nor any cause, neither fascist nor antifascist, nor communist, nor patriot. He would work for anyone, le Baron said. After the war he ended up in one of those little border towns in Eastern Europe where anyone could sell or buy anything, including passports and new identities. Somewhere along the way he got a press pass and a uniform. Cuban, le Baron thought, or Paraguayan, with a badge, papers, and calling card.

"Uniforms counted for a great deal back then," le Baron said. "So did papers. He was free to move anywhere."

"How do you know all this?" I asked. "Is he a friend?"

"He told me."

Le Baron said that half of what Dushko told anybody was probably a front, but that he didn't make it up entirely. "Part of his story must be true," he said. "He was always in and out of international trade, for example. But he was a good forger of documents, and he was also dealing in contraband. He managed to get himself down to Monte Carlo at some point with money in his pocket, and he was intelligent enough to win some earnings for a while. He may even have worked out a system to beat the wheel."

Le Baron was living in Nice at the time and used to see Dushko around. He was either rich or destitute. Never in between.

"Once when I saw him he was living in a tent in a gypsy camp outside Nice. Next time I saw him he was in a tuxedo at the bar at the Negresco."

I took a chance and asked how it came to pass that he knew such a man as Dushko. Le Baron claimed that he had been

working in a bank in Nice and that Dushko had come in to fill
out an application for a loan.

"The documentation was suspect. We could see that immediately, but for some reason, I liked him. He was such a good
talker, such a great posturing liar, and he had all those stories. He
could go on for hours with his tales of intrigue. He could talk or
buy his way out of anything, I daresay. Even Nazi prisons. We
had lunch one day and he pulled a card trick to see who would
pick up the chit. I played, knowing what I was getting into, and
he won, as I knew he would, of course. He amused me. Then he
began to pester me, and then I dropped him. And now here he is
again."

"He wants money?"

"Dushko does not come looking for you to make social calls,"
he said.

He drained his beer and looked around for a waiter.

"I must be going," he said and left some coins on the table,
more than enough to cover my beer as well as his, I noticed.

We shook hands.

"I say, would you like to come out to the villa some evening for
dinner?" he asked. "Bring your little friend with you. She might
enjoy the garden. I happen to know she is not unfamiliar with
country houses."

The invitation was a little frightening, but I said I would like
to come sometime if Jean-Pierre would liberate me from my
dreaded scullery.

He laughed again. "Of course he will," he said. "I'll mention
it to him."

On another one of my free days, after a long nap I took a stroll out to the Ile de la Pietra to the Genoese tower. I hiked north-ward out over the red battlements of rocks and threaded my way between narrow passages to the isolated north shore of the islet. The ancient Genoese tower loomed above me like a judge, and in time I came to a blue-green, narrow cove. It was dead still and hot that day, and rather than smashing itself apart on the rocks as it often did in this exposed quarter, the smooth water simply rose and fell quietly, as if the sea were breathing. I stripped and dove in and floated there, dreaming of the vast sweep of human history that engulfed this part of the world — the old Torréens who built the menhirs and torri scattered around the island, the Phoeni-cian traders nosing into the coves along the coast, the Greeks in their dark-prowed galleys, Romans in their cataphract triremes, Genoese, English, and French — and all of them warring with one another. Alone there, surrounded by the silent sky and the slow rise and fall of the quiet sea, I could almost hear somewhere in the distance the clash of bronze swords and the shouts of wave on wave of senseless armies hammering at each other — and to what end? "A quoi bon?" as Marie's tutor Giancarlo used to say during his vast reviews of human history.

Back on shore I dried off in the sun and carried on with my exploration, intending to circle the islet and return to my cottage on the little causeway. I was forced inland in some sections, and had to clamber up through narrow passages and then work my way back down to the shore. Halfway around, at the western end of the islet, I was once again forced upward, and on my way back down from the heights, I could see down to the flat, smooth-rock shore that ran out to the west. Here I saw a couple lounging, a blond woman stretched out flat and a sandy-haired man on his side, propped on his right elbow and leaning over the woman intimately. They were both nude and had been for a swim. I could see the gleam of water on their skin and their wet hair.

It was a bit of a shock. I recognized André and Maggs.

So as not to intrude I retreated, climbed over the top of the island, passed under the Genoese watchtower, and rested there for a while, my heart pounding.

I knew that adults had affairs; illicit assignations were not uncommon in the New York suburb where I had grown up; and there were constant flirtations and affairs at the Rose Café. But this was somehow different. If it had been Chrétien with Karen, someone my age, I would have been amused. I had seen Maggs taking a coffee or a glass of beer with André and had seen them sometimes leaning close together in intimate conversation and dancing together when the gypsies were at the café. But I was too naive to realize that they were beginning an affair.

Be that as it may, when I saw her the next day, Maggs joined me on the terrace and carried on as if nothing had occurred over the past week that was in any way different from any other seven-day period. She chattered on about Poland and London, and the color of the sea beyond the harbor and that funny little man Pierrot, with his cocked eye and his down-at-heel espadrilles. The difference was in me, I realized, and I began to listen to her war stories in a new way, trying to work out an explanation for her betrayal of Peter. I had a dull, unformed thought that Peter was a bit of a bore, a quiet sort, with an obsession for spearfishing. On the other hand, he had to have something within him. I gathered from what Maggs had said that he was a fairly successful sculptor back in London, and I had heard that he had traveled around India on a motorcycle in his younger years.

I sensed all along that something worse than the average horror of war-torn Warsaw was haunting Maggs. She often mentioned a certain Nazi officer in her stories of her Warsaw youth. She had spoken of him so often I began to wonder if she had perhaps been his girlfriend, and in fact once I ventured to merely hint at asking her in as indirect a manner as I could summon. But with her seemingly instinctive ability to read character and thoughts, she must have seen it coming and dodged the question before I was even able to launch it. She went on to speak of the officer's many qualities: I gather he was older, and, at least in her view (she must have been about seventeen), worldly and civilized, fluent in languages, knew all about ancient Greece, and used to quote long passages from Friedrich Hölderlin to her. He could also play the piano.

"Once I was with him in a little bistro when no one was around," she said. "He saw a piano. 'Ah ha,' he said. 'Please excuse me for one moment.' He went over, sat down, and played a few little Mozart passages. Then he rested a minute, rubbed his hands together, and set into the opening bars of Bach's *Goldberg Variations*. He must have been studying for years ..."

She drew a breath and looked out at the harbor.

"But then one day when I was with him on the street, we came suddenly upon a Jewish family ..."

She halted, glanced up at me quickly, and then looked back at the ice at the bottom of her glass.

Just then one of the martins flitted past us and landed in its nest, fluttering. The young pitched their heads up and began squawking, open-beaked. She looked over at them.

"You know, sometimes I think that human beings are an aberration of nature, an evolutionary dead end that will end up exterminating itself by its own hand," she said. "The animals are more ethical than we are, don't you think? They have a code that they live by. They don't just kill indiscriminately. But we, we have no purpose. None that I can tell, anyway."

She shifted her glass on the table, brushed back her hair from her eyes, and stopped talking.

The silence was ominous.

"Where's Peter today?" I asked.

"Oh you know, out with Jean-Pierre probably. Spearfishing. The usual." She sipped her beer. "I wish I could do that," she said. "I'm getting restless out here. I think I need to get back to London and work."

chapter thirteen Le Baron

For some reason, the theoretical dinner invitation from le Baron made me nervous. I was half-hoping he'd forget about it. But a few days later, when he came out for a card game, he mentioned it again.

By this time, even though I had been snooping around all summer long, I didn't feel I knew any more about le Baron than when I first saw him making his way across the town square in his white linen suit back in April. Furthermore, all the conflicting stories about him were mounting.

One of the most entertaining came from Marie not long after le Baron first floated his invitation. We had taken a walk out to the Genoese tower on one of my afternoons off, and we came to the flat rock at the western end of the island and decided to swim out to the little rocky islet called la Brochetta.

We slipped into the water and swam across the channel, fighting a rip all along the way, and then after a rest, swam back. Marie was a strong swimmer and got there first, and she clambered up over the rocks like some elemental, glistening sea creature. We found a flat place and lay back in the sun, drying off.

It was another one of those still, moist days when the sea was calm and green, and the silvery gulls and terns were criss-crossing the island just above the tower and the red-rock heights. Marie picked a sprig of the curry-scented immortelle and began smelling it and running it over her cheeks. I could smell the pungent scent from where I lay — curry mixed with the odor of dried seaweed and saltwater.

She was talking about Paris again and how profoundly boring her tutor was becoming and how the summer was wearing
on — all subjects I had heard about before. I was growing drowsy
and must have drifted off to her rising and falling monologue.
Then in my somnolent state, I became aware that the chatter
had stopped and the scent of immortelle had intensified. I felt an
insect on my upper lip and brushed it away. Marie was leaning
over me, tickling me with the flower.

"And so, as I was saying to you, that night le Baron tried to
seduce me on the beach, but I managed to resist," she said.

"Don't joke," I said. "Did you know that he has invited us to
dinner?"

She threw down the sprig of immortelle dramatically.

"Oh *mon Dieu,* no. Too dangerous. We should not go. He is a
very bad man. I have heard this now from my parents."

Now she had managed to get my interest. I sat up.

"What? What did they say? Is he a drug runner? Something
to do with the *Bagheera?*"

"Maybe. They looked him up."

"Guns," I said. "He runs guns into Algeria. He supplies the
OAS with plastique."

"'No. Not guns. No bombs," she said.

"Drugs? Hashish?"

"No. Worse."

"Tell me," I said.

"Give a kiss first."

I kissed her.

"Again," she said.

"Tell me first."

"Kiss me. Don't cowboys like to kiss girls?"

"He's a bank robber," I said. "A swindler. He works with that Dushko. They've transferred stolen, ill-gotten funds to Switzerland."

She leaned back on her elbows and looked me in the eye.

"Do you know that you are a truly dimwitted cowboy?" she said.

She sat up, grabbed the hair on the back of my head, pushed me down, and kissed me.

"So this Baron, what did they say?" I persisted.

She straightened up again, tousled her hair, and sighed.

"OK. You want to know. I will tell you. My parents, they said he was mixed up in a gang."

"Really?"

"Yes, really. A terrible gang of murderers."

"Le Baron?"

"Yes. Do you know what they would do during the war? They would go out at night. People were hungry then; there was not enough to eat. So le Baron and his gang, they would go out at night and catch children, cook them up, and eat them. Le Baron invented some savory dishes, which he would sell in the markets. Young boy *aux fines herbes* stewed in wine and eau-de-vie. It was one of his favorites. He used to eat American soldiers too, the fat ones . . ."

I kissed her.

"Now tell me," I said.

"I did, it's true. It's what my parents told me."

"If he ate American soldiers," I said, "I am going to have to eat you in revenge. I learned from American soldiers how to eat French girls."

She slapped me and headed for the water.

By this time in the season, the younger crowd there — Chrétien, Karen and her family, Marie, and a shy, mousy French colonial girl who was a refugee from Indochina — had formed a small society of sorts. Periodically, if Chrétien and I could get free, we would all go out to the Ile de la Pietra to swim off the rocks. They all knew about le Baron. Karen and Clotilde had noticed him, of course, since he was a type they had seen often on the Riviera and around the Champs Elysées, and Laurent was very interested in his style of dress, although he had, on several occasions, pronounced it sadly out of fashion. "Too English," he said.

Among this group, the theories as to le Baron's livelihood and origin ranged widely around the fringes of the various métiers of the European underworld. He was a Russian spy. He was a police undercover agent, gathering information on Pierre Corsini's family of known contrabandists. He made his money selling stolen Jewish-owned art after the war. He smuggled guns and plastique to Oran and Algiers for the FLN. He was involved in illegal shipments of adulterated wine to Cap Corse. He was mixed up in land scandals in Saint-Tropez, where he ran a ring of prostitutes. Or alternatively, from Marie (again), he was a known smuggler of white slaves.

The most entertaining theory (apart from Marie's version) came from an unlikely source — Laurent.

"I have it on good authority," he said smugly, "that he was a priest."

Laurent said that le Baron, before he was le Baron, had a big church in Nice with many loyal parishioners. But for years he had dipped into the ample church treasury. On the side he supported a beautiful dusky mistress, an African princess.

One night, according to Laurent's sources, he was discovered with her in flagrante by his curate, who blackmailed him. The curate found out later that he was also stealing from the coffers and upped his fee, so le Baron cashed out the entire church savings and fled. He assumed the most unlikely new identity he could think of, a German baron, and decamped with his African princess to Corsica, where he knew no questions would be asked.

A more serious, albeit still outrageous theory came from Chrétien, who had been privy to all my own private investigations and theories.

"It's so obvious," he said. "So clear you don't even think of it — he's in the OAS. All those anti-Gaullist generals and colonels are in flight now from the French secret police. They're all in hiding in out-of-the-way places. He's one of them. He has big financial interests in northern France and he's financing all the attempts to assassinate de Gaulle."

"Doesn't fit," I pointed out. "Everyone agrees he's been out here since the Second World War. He never was in Algeria, nor the military, and he's not that type anyway. Those guys don't wear tailored linen suits. Furthermore, he's supposed to be Belgian. Why would he care?"

"He's not Belgian. He just tells people that."

I had heard that many of the agents who were associated with the secret police and the anti-OAS agencies were Corsican, some of them from the Corsican underworld that worked out of Marseille and Paris. It made no sense that an OAS operative would hide in the midst of his known enemies. I said as much to Chrétien.

"The fox sets up house in the kennel, don't you see?" he said.
"Who told you all this, anyway?"
"Micheline. She knows all about him. They had an affair last
winter. The pillow speaks the truth."

My more acceptable sources as to the Baron's livelihood were no
less helpful in the end. Jean-Pierre corroborated most of what
Micheline had told me about le Baron. His family had lost their
big château to the Nazis during the war and moved down to
Paris. But he added that during the war le Baron had hooked
up with a German count who had also been turned out, and had
been put under house arrest near Baden-Baden. The count fled
and came down to Nice, where he met le Baron. They began a
collaboration in which they provided forged papers for people.
They might even have been connected with one of the various
plots to kill Hitler.

Max claimed le Baron was involved in contraband, something
to do with the *Bagheera*. Vincenzo said he was a banker with
possible black-market dealings. André and Micheline thought
he had underworld connections.

In all these various permutations of his career, no matter how
varied, there was a singular French term that came up regularly.
Le Baron was *un brasseur d'affaires*, a high-level financier with
possible shady connections.

Only Claude, the barber, dismissed all the contraband and
criminal connections as mere gossip. He said that le Baron was a
man of honor, and he did not, when he said this, intend the local
term, *bandit d'honneur*, which is the Corsican phrase for someone who has committed a justifiable crime, such as a vendetta.

At least I don't think he did. Claude said le Baron was simply a well-connected banker from a good family who had realized some success and retired to Ile Rousse, and nothing more.

"Out here, if anybody from the continent comes along with a little money through honest labor, anyone who betters himself, they say he is a criminal, part of the Marseille underworld, the milieu. Not true with le Baron. Believe me, he is an upstanding man. He helped out my mother. She was very sick with a bad heart. He flew her to the hospital in Nice and he wouldn't even hear of it when I said I would pay him back."

He had long before dismissed Fabrizio's tale.

"Fabrizio is just one of those people who was undone by the war, although he never was much of anything to begin with, I should say. He was in the resistance in a way; that is, he knew people, and maquisards would come up to his compound to hide arms around the forest there. The Nazis used to come and beat him up as a matter of course to try to get him to inform. He never talked, but he's never been the same. Did he tell you he killed a lot of Germans?"

"Yes, he implied that he had."

"Fabrizio doesn't even like to slaughter a chicken. That's why there are so many old useless donkeys around his place. He can't bring himself to shoot them."

We were discussing all this in our usual spot at the town square.

Out on the boule pitch beyond the café, there was a short outburst of cheers. Someone had made a good throw.

"Fabrizio told me that there was money in his family," I said.

"But yes, that much is true," Claude said. "He did come from an old family. He likes to tell people that he is a signori, one of the direct descendants of the old feudal lords of Corsica. He's one of these landed country types who lives like a pauper but has money stashed all over the place. I've never seen this, but they say he has buried silver around the property and under the haymows. Never spends anything, though."

"They also said he is a mazzero," I said.

Claude snickered. "Don't believe that. That's back in the old days. There are no mazzeri around here on this coast. Maybe somewhere in the south. But this is the new Corsica up here. Tourists come. Germans, our old adversaries. Swedes. We're going to be part of the new Europe here. And it's a good thing, too. Good for business. I like the Germans. I like the Parisians. I like le Baron. Look at Jean-Pierre and Micheline. They're foreign. We're all one now. We should not be so autonomist."

The boules players re-formed for a new game. One of them threw the cochonnet for the next round. An old man in black corduroy took the first throw.

"You want to know why all these people say bad things about le Baron?" Claude said. "I will tell you. It is because they have nothing. They do nothing. They play cards. Pitch boules. Work — if they work at all — just enough to get by, no more. And some of them are shady characters themselves. I can tell you. In my position in this community, I hear things. But le Baron. He worked in banks. He came from a good family, generous, benevolent. He has maintained himself with honor."

The first throw struck the cochonnet and sent it spinning off.

A chorus of exclamation.

Gulls crossed over the plaza, screeching. Children skipped around the little carousel at the west end in front of the bank. Dogs. A drunk man. Women in print dresses in a loose circle, gossiping. Shouts from the market.

Claude said he had to leave, but before he stood up, a flight of sparrows flitted in. He broke off a hunk of bread and tossed it to them, and they scrambled for it, some chasing the others off to defend their crumbs.

He was halfway across the plaza when I saw him stop for a second. Then he turned around and came shuffling back, sat down, and pulled his chair over next to mine so that he was only a few feet away. He leaned toward me.

"You know, there is one thing more I know about le Baron. I think he told me, because — you know — my condition. And maybe because of the troubles with my mother.

"Do you know that Dushko fellow who's out here looking for le Baron? They were in prison together. Some Vichy types, they don't like people like le Baron. They turned him in to the Nazis and he was taken up to Berlin and held in an underground prison cell there, in solitary confinement. They tortured him. He knew nothing. He could not have talked if he wanted to. He was outside the main networks and resistance cells, just a supplier and a forger of documents to those fighting the Nazis. He did not know the leaders they were hunting for, and they knew that, but they tortured him anyway. He and Dushko. Dushko, he maybe had information; he was widely traveled in the underground. But not le Baron. He maintained his honor throughout, I tell you. He doesn't like to talk about that period in his life. He doesn't want to remember that. Somehow the two of them got out, I think due to Dushko's efforts. They paid off guards. Le Baron came out here to nurse his wounds. Dushko disappeared into Eastern Europe."

He stood and patted my shoulder again.

"Just don't worry. Let it go. Le Baron probably wouldn't want you to know that sort of thing about him."

I watched him limp off through the plaza.

I had to wonder about this story, just as I had questioned all the others. They were all buzz and chatter, like the meaningless cheeps and whistles of the birds in the maquis. Fact and inventive fictions; contrasts, legends, lies, and gossip; and maybe somewhere in all the stories, a little bit of truth that one could never really determine.

Walking back from town that afternoon I began to wonder why I even cared. Le Baron had always been nice to me, seemingly accessible and appreciative, or at least bemused by my uneventful sojourn in this place. The truth is, I suppose, he represented for me the old Europe, with all its style, class, elegance, and refinements, as well as its corruption, vice, violence, and world-weary cynicism — all of which I had originally come to Europe to experience. Whoever le Baron was, whatever he had done or had not done, he was a true native of the European continent. He was part of an ancient lineage out of the caves of Périgord, nursed for generations through century after century of plagues, famines, wars, inquisitions, and a thousand years of murderous regimes that had ended only fifteen years earlier, in what amounted to the greatest singular atrocity ever carried out by one group of human beings upon another. Le Baron was a survivor. He endured.

The following week, while I was having a drink at the same table in the plaza, I saw Maggs coming out from the little temple-like market stalls across the square. She was carrying a net bag with some fruit and was wearing one of her short, brightly colored skirts and blue espadrilles. I watched her circle the square. She was in no hurry, merely strolling along, pausing briefly to look in shop windows and then moving on. She stood out among the dark-haired masses: blond, very trim, and wearing her loud colors. I noticed men in the cafés on the other side of the square turning to watch as she passed.

When she arrived at my side of the plaza I called out to her, and she joined me at the table.

"What are you doing here?" she asked.

"I'm hiding from Vincenzo," I said. "There is a mess of fish back there to clean, potatoes to peel, onions to chop."

She order a demi of beer and we watched the action on the square. The boules players were forming a new game.

"They come here every afternoon," I told her. "The same old men."

"This must be their way of ordering their world," she said. "People now do not have that so much anymore, the old ways."

She sipped her beer and looked at them again.

From the first time I saw her, she had reminded me of someone I thought I knew, but watching her here, out of context, I realized that she looked like the American actress Eva Marie Saint — high cheekbones, winsome blue eyes, blond hair.

With the lines formed, the small man called Henri took up his boule and made the first cast. It was a modestly good throw, and there arose among the assembled a dull chorus of approval. Another made his pitch, a wide shot that generated no comment. And then another. And then a fourth.

Maggs looked back at me.

"They do this every day, don't they?"

"Heavy rain keeps them in," I said. "But not wind."

Just then the one-armed man took up his post. The mumbling of the chorus softened. He scraped away a few stones with his left foot. Stood eyeing the cochonnet, bowed, tipped his arm, and threw. The boule swept over the pitch, angled down, and nestled against the little pig. A kiss. A palpable kiss.

"That's Robespierre," I told Maggs. "He's the best of the lot here."

"Robespierre is his name?"

"Yes, the barber told me that. He was a leader of an underground network around here. Lost his arm in an ambush on an armored car. Robespierre was his code name. They all had code names. That little man with the squinty eyes was known as Mouse, but they don't call him that anymore."

"What do you do?" she asked. "Come down here all the time and watch? How do you know all this?"

I told her that on certain days I would come here in the late afternoon, take a drink, and watch the action on the square, but on other days I would go out to the Ile de la Pietra to the tower, and at other times I would hitch a ride and take a hike in the maquis, alone. I realized as soon as I said it that she might suspect that I had spotted her with André. But it was too late.

"What a life," she said.

"Yes, but I also have to clean fish every day and get pricked by rascasse spines." I showed her my swollen thumb.

"You know, it's odd," she said. "I saw you sitting here, and I felt a flash of something, maybe it was just recognition but maybe something else. You look more natural here. I see you more as you are, perhaps. You do know that we're on to your trick, don't you? You play at being that dimwitted busboy who shuffles out from the kitchen in his stained apron and sweeps the floors or cleans fish and pretends not to know what's going on. But I see you listening. I see you pretending not to understand French or even English when you want. Speaking in Italian with Vincenzo. You are more than they all think you are, aren't you?"

"Well, cleaning fish was never my ambition, exactly — I don't think."

"What is?" she asked bluntly.

This stopped me. Except for my vague, as-yet-inactivated idea of becoming a writer, like many people of my time, I had given up on words like ambition, career, and duty.

I said as much to her.

"But that's quite enough, really, that's perfect. You should just write and don't worry about duty and conviction. You don't need to be certain. You don't need to believe. That's one of the things I learned in Warsaw, isn't it, not to believe in anything. The Nazis believed. The Jews believed. And look what happened. Don't bother to believe in any one thing. Just go ahead and write."

She reached over and patted my wrist. Then she rested her hand on mine for a second, and then she squeezed and patted my hand again, looking me in the eye.

"You are an engaging young man," she said, still resting her hand on mine.

She had that same steady look that le Baron had — a direct, unblinking stare that seemed to have the ability to penetrate and expose any element of untruth in what you said. It was a look that made me nervous, and, coming from her, with her warm hand still on mine, I wondered — briefly — if I was perhaps being propositioned. I didn't know what to say.

"Never mind," she said. "I've got to go. Peter will be coming back from his spearfishing, and he'll be wondering where I am again."

She stood. Then, smiling sadly, she said something in Polish. I didn't dare ask her to translate.

chapter fourteen

The Dinner Party

$\dagger$

The dinner invitation came through after all, as I feared it would. Jean-Pierre mentioned, almost casually, that le Baron had invited me and Marie to come out for an informal evening at his villa.

"You can take the night off. Take the car."

Marie was sitting in the nook with Giancarlo, swinging her right leg nervously and pretending to pay attention. She glanced over at me. I think she knew what we were talking about.

"Marie knows?"

"Yes, I told her."

For all my interest in le Baron, I was not entirely happy about this upcoming event and went around the rest of the day killing time and not enjoying myself very much. I didn't look forward to a whole evening with this formal old gentleman and his penetrating blue eyes. It seemed like work to me, even though I was genuinely curious to learn more about his life. By that time in the season, anything that even remotely resembled something out of the ordinary line of work displeased me. I liked my unadventurous routine of sweeping floors, clearing tables, and cleaning fish and dishes. I liked my afternoon hours in the town or my rambles in the maquis or the hot sojourns on the rocks of the Ile de la Pietra. I didn't want anything to interrupt the routine.

I talked to Marie later that afternoon about our upcoming date, and she said she felt the same way.

"I don't like it," she said. "I think he has designs. I don't know what. We must be on guard."

"Max told me he just likes younger people," I said.

"Yes, of course, but why?"

For all her youth and chatter and professed Catholicism, Marie was not naive.

After I cleaned the fish for the evening meal, I went for a swim in the cove, then dressed in a clean shirt, and went to the bar, where I sat fortifying myself with a glass of wine, waiting for Marie.

As usual, just before the dinner hour she made her grand entrance at the door. She was dressed in a light silk blouse and a dark skirt and big hooped earrings. I noticed that she had made a point of wearing her small silver crucifix necklace and that she had buttoned her blouse higher up on her chest than she usually did. The ruse didn't work, though. Even if she had gone in disguise as a nun, any experienced older lecher such as le Baron — if that's what he was — could spot the coiled sexuality beneath the habit by her walk alone.

"Ready?" I asked her.

She signed herself in jest.

Jean-Pierre's car was an old black Citroën with red leather seats. It was too big a car for me, too grand, I felt, but I got in and managed, after some fiddling, to get it started. I backed out onto the causeway from the parking area, shifted gears, and drove slowly down the road, bouncing on the ruts and stones as we moved. I was dreading navigation of this excellent chariot through the maze of back streets of Ile Rousse, not to mention the narrow, winding, donkey-blocked road that ran toward the village of Santa-Reparata and le Baron's villa. But I forged on.

About a half-mile beyond the village, just where the maquis began, we turned off on a side track and jounced down a rocky road. Below us was the straight, cypress-lined drive that led to the villa. We drove in and parked in the courtyard on the left side of the house. A scruffy, one-eyed man dressed in worker's blues was in the yard, raking. He must have been mute, since he merely indicated the door with a sign and then led us to it, knocked on it for us, and backed away. A dark-eyed maid with a 1940s hairdo and a white apron opened the door, eyed us, and then guided us through the hallway to another set of French doors opening onto a garden behind the house.

"He's out there someplace," she said. "You'll find him."

There was a raked-earth path leading to a fountain, and in one of the side gardens off the main allée, among the tea roses, we saw le Baron. He was dressed in pressed khaki trousers, a white collared shirt and a paisley cravat, and a houndstooth jacket — dressed down on this occasion, for our sakes perhaps. He advanced enthusiastically, his hand outstretched, his smooth, tanned face shining. He kissed Marie on each cheek, and then gathered up her hands and kissed them, laughing.

"Two young roses," he said, speaking in French. I don't know whether he meant Marie's hands or the two of us.

"Please," he said, spreading his right hand back to the garden.

A woman appeared during our greeting and stood in the middle of one of the paths. She seemed horrified at our presence at first, wordless, as if we were invaders, her big china-blue eyes wide and her hand at her throat.

"May I present," said le Baron, "my wife, Isabelle."

Her apparent surprise dissipated, and she approached and took my hand warmly and then kissed Marie on both cheeks, as if they knew each other.

She had ash-blond hair and smooth, papery skin, delicate

hands and well-manicured nails, and she was dressed in a simple white blouse, a small gold necklace, and pearl earrings. I would have said she was about forty-five, but she was one of those women whose age cannot be determined.

After small talk, we moved to a terrace by the French doors, and the maid brought out a silver tray with a bottle of Heidsieck — a 1959, I noticed, a vintage year that everyone was talking about at that time. She came back out with a plate of fresh crudités and olives, which she set down on the filigreed iron garden table.

Le Baron poured the champagne. We toasted America; we toasted a safer world; we said we were all worried about Nikita; and we all laughed heartily at this double entendre because we all knew this was the name of the lazy dog belonging to Jean-Pierre and Micheline, but that there was, over in Russia, another Nikita who bore watching, as le Baron said, and on and on, and le Baron was at his most *charmant*, winking and smiling to Marie and back to his wife, and leaping up to help with the service, and bowing and scraping and acting young at heart in the company of such young blood, such fresh young roses, as he said.

As the champagne sank lower in the bottle, we all began to relax, another bottle, another '59, appeared and soon Marie, who was not a heavy drinker, was chatting on about her stupid parents and their stupid political views. Le Baron and Isabelle laughed warmly at her monologue, and then, Isabelle — as she insisted I call her — cornered me privately and asked me all about my studies and why had I chosen France, and did I like the current president, John Kennedy, and then the maid appeared again and dinner was announced.

We went indoors through the airy main foyer, and through a formal dining room to a conservatory on the south side of the house, where the table was laid with crystal and silver and Limoges dinner plates. The glass doors to the conservatory were flung open, and as dusk fell I could hear the ringing chirp of crickets and night birds in the garden tangle beyond the more formal garden rooms. It was a sound I was not used to in my sea-eagle aerie above the cove, and it spoke of moist luxuriance, of fecund life, with a hint of savagery.

Dinner began with a light fish broth that tasted of fennel and orange, served with a local white malvoisie wine. Following this, there was a serving of several small cakes of pâté. Isabelle identified each one as the plate was passed: a pâté of rouget, another of rabbit, and another of *merle*, the local blackbird. Then came the main course, a succulent dish of partridges cooked with white grapes and wine. Le Baron had a little discussion with the maid in patois, and she came back with a bottle of wine, which le Baron himself opened and tasted first.

I didn't know wines that well, but I knew enough to notice that it was a Montrachet, also 1959.

We carried on with our political discussion in a lighthearted manner. They seemed to be interested in what we, the younger generation, thought of all that was going on: Algeria liberated, the right wing on the rampage in Paris, John Kennedy and Cuba, Nikita Khrushchev in Russia, Indochina, and the American advisors now loosed in Vietnam in the wake of the French failures. They had picked the wrong people to ask; along with Herr Komandante, we were the least political players around the Rose Café. But this did not stop Marie from contributing her opinions. In the main, she was tired of the Arabs.

"In Paris now, you cannot go into the parks. Some dirty Arab man will come by and ask you to go to bed with him, and when you ignore him he persists, and you have to get up and find another place. And no sooner are you seated than another dirty man comes by."

"Oh, but this is so disturbing," Isabelle said in sympathy. "I do not think I would enjoy Paris anymore."

Le Baron remained silent but shook his head and clucked, as if to say that this is the sad course of history but that worse things could be happening.

I tried to spot Isabelle's accent. It sounded like upper-class Parisian to me, with that high, ascending, cracked voice at the end of each phrase. Le Baron's French, which I had never heard for any length of time, since he usually spoke English with me, did not seem to me to have any particular inflection — none that I could recognize, in any case.

The partridge dish was cleared, and the maid brought out a plain green salad and a couple of bottles of sparkling water, and the conversation turned to local intrigues, mainly the noisy fights of Vincenzo and Lucretia, André and Jacquis and the nightly card game, and Pierre Corsini (the man they call Moonface) and his notoriously bad family, who were always in some scrape or another. Then le Baron told a few stories of famous bandit families of Corsica who lived long ago in the mountains and who still were legendary.

"Fortunately, those days are over now," le Baron said.

I wanted to ask if they knew of Pierrot's old father Fabrizio, but given Fabrizio's version of le Baron's history, I was afraid to bring it up.

The salad was cleared and a plate of cheeses appeared: a sheep's cheese called *bastilicacciu*, a soft goat cheese, and a hard, somewhat sharp cow's cheese.

Then the dessert was served. It was a *fiadone*, a local specialty made with pureed brocciu that had been soaked in spirits and was flamed at the table by the maid just before it was served.

Over dessert and a bottle of Cap Corse muscat, le Baron entertained us with a long, tedious story of a fishing expedition he made once with Jean-Pierre, who had tried to teach him to spearfish. They had taken a boat around to one of the coves to the east, toward Cap Corse. But while they were out the libeccio picked up, and they couldn't get back. They had to leave the boat, hike up to a small collection of houses on the hillside, and hitchhike back to town in their bathing suits and sailor's jerseys. I think the humor of the story arose from self-mockery; le Baron was not accustomed to such deshabille.

Following this, the maid brought coffee, four tiny glasses, and a bottle of Hospices de Beaune marc, which, le Baron commented, was not easy to obtain in those times and had been purchased at an auction. He offered around Gitanes, and Marie, who did not normally smoke, accepted one and coughed — I think she was fairly well lubricated at this point. In the brief interlude of Marie's coughing, le Baron said something sotto voce to his wife.

It crossed my mind that these two were plotting something and that they were both opium addicts or *hashishiens* and were going to bring out a pipe next. But maybe that was the result of too much le Baron gossip.

The marc was poured, formally, by le Baron. The air grew closer. The odor of the garden and the maquis filtered through the windows. I could smell eglantine and arbutus, roses, and the cinnamon-flavored scent of stock. The cricket calls increased and throbbed with a belling, rhythmic pulse, and far off, somewhere in the greeny tangle beyond the gardens, a nightingale poured out a single phrase.

Marie excused herself to visit the bathroom. She rose from the table and steadied herself with her left hand on the back of the chair while Isabelle gave her directions. She was still able to maintain her poise, however, and I saw le Baron watch her disappear down through the rooms, her white blouse growing dimmer and dimmer as she moved through the passageways.

I could tell she was drunk. She had relaxed her balletic grace and was moving casually, her hips swaying.

"She is very lovely, your friend," Isabelle said in English. "I know of her parents. You must be careful if you meet them sometime up in Paris. They will draw you in. They're very political, you know. The right wing hates them, both of them. And Marie, too, she should be careful, she seems so fragile, so innocent."

Le Baron chuckled privately, as if he knew something that Isabelle did not know, but that I probably did know. Isabelle caught his drift.

"*Mais non, Edouard*," she said. "She is a rose. The last rose of summer."

Le Baron leaned toward me, smiling conspiratorially. "My wife," he said to me, "she is, you understand, a lost romantic. She lives for beauty. And a young woman such as your Marie ..." He gestured in the direction of the hall she had passed through and nodded slowly.

"Who wouldn't want only roses?" Isabelle said. "You've seen what we have seen."

"I gather," I said, seeing an opening. "It must have been terrible in these parts during the war years. I've read about it a little. But we were so isolated from it all in America. It seems unreal, you know, unless you were a soldier."

"Or a mother," Isabelle said.

Marie returned, and the curtain closed again. But it opened later in the evening when Marie herself launched into another one of her requisite anticommunist lectures. Her father's car had been blown up that winter by some right-wing terrorist group, probably the OAS, but Marie was decidedly reactionary and was unafraid to offer her generally unexamined opinions. Her views, outrageous though they seemed to me, were entertaining to our hosts.

The evening slowly wound down, and at a lull in the conversation Isabelle offered to show Marie an antique pearl necklace that had belonged to someone in the Bonaparte family. Le Baron asked if I would like to take a stroll around the garden.

"Your little friend Marie," le Baron said, once we were alone, "she really is very energetic. Older people such as Isabelle and I, we enjoy very much that energy, no matter how it is directed. Isabelle loves the flowers, the fresh cheeks of youth. She is shy, you understand. We live alone out here, and she prefers to remain here, reading and sketching flowers."

We walked on and turned down one of the axis paths. He had a lighted cigarette, which he carried between his thumb and forefinger and smoked reflectively whenever we stopped.

"Isabelle has few friends out here. Me, she knows of course. Ten years now we have been together, and as you may know, or will perhaps learn someday, certain things wear thin after a few years."

He drew on his cigarette.

"Familiarity, I suppose. But you, you must have a good time with Marie. She favors you, I can tell."

I could see where we were headed and tried to cut him off.

"Actually no," I said to le Baron. "Did you know that Marie is a devout Catholic? It's probably a reaction to her parents; she says they're atheists. She gives me speeches. She's a virgin and she says that she intends to remain that way until she is married."

Le Baron sighed. "Are you sure about that?" he asked.

He glanced over at me with those blue-flame eyes and paused briefly. In the pause, I changed the subject.

"One of the things I have been doing in Paris is following the stories of the war," I said (only partly true). "It must have been dangerous here in the south as well."

"It was the jungle," he said bitterly.

"Let's take another drink," he said, and guided me back to the garden table.

He fetched the marc and poured two glasses and offered me a cigarette.

"Listen, I happen to know you are very curious about my livelihood and background," he said.

I must have reddened and he must have spotted it even in the shadowy light. He chuckled.

"C'est normal," he said. "But you and your journalistic dogged-ness. I knew journalists in Paris. As you may know, in all stories there may be some truth," he said. "But there are often some very great lies."

Le Baron said he knew what I had been hearing, and that there was an element of truth to some of it. He said he thought when he had a beer with me down in the town that day that he should really just have set me straight, but decided to wait for a time when he could explain more fully. That's when he thought to have me out to dinner.

The money, "what is left of it," he said, was his family's money. They had a big estate outside of Charles le Roi in Belgium, even though he lived mostly in Paris and spent much of his youth there. He had been to school in England and still had friends in London when the war came. He was fluent in English by that time and was thinking of fleeing to England, but was contacted in Paris by the security service and was encouraged to stay on in France. Early on, his family estate had been taken over as a Nazi command center, as Micheline had said, and his parents and two sisters fled to Paris where they had an apartment. He remained in Paris, ostensibly working at a banking firm, but collecting information on money transactions and verifying who was being watched by the Gestapo and who was not being watched. He would then convey the news to other operatives, who would somehow radio the information to the British. Or so he thought. He claimed that he really didn't know what happened once he transferred the information.

He said he was basically a peaceable man and did not want to get any more deeply involved in the underground. "It could only lead to killing," he said, and he didn't think he could live with that. So he quit the service, after some negotiation managed to get a pass to Nice, where he melted into the background. He moved up to Vence, behind Nice, but with the known world falling apart around him, he grew restless and contacted the underground networks again to see if there was anything he could do to help without getting deeply involved. The network head — or one of them, "you never knew who was who, in that world," he said — asked him to help arrange documents for people. The

Vichy government, at Berlin's request, was deporting Jews by this time.

"We all know this now. But back then it was less clear, unless you were a Jew, of course, although even then some of the richer Jewish families refused to believe it. You could easily pretend that you didn't know what was going on, you see. Don't ask, don't pry. It's why I like your questions. You are not afraid to ask questions. So many of us preferred not to ask."

He finished off his glass, stared at it for a minute, and then looked out at the black garden. I could see one of the white rose trees glowing in the sultry night. The crickets were pulsing in the shrubbery. A dog barked from one of the neighboring farms. I kept my mouth shut.

"It can be dangerous, though, too many questions. Even now, there is a certain danger," he said.

After another short silence, he resumed.

In Nice he joined an underground forgery ring and learned to fake documents, and in time was able to arrange papers for families. He knew some Jewish families with big villas up behind the city and was able to help them. Then he began to help people who were living in the loosely guarded internment camps and still had family members on the outside — children, wives, and old grandmothers. He arranged false exit visas and letters of passage out through the Pyrenees into Spain, or outbound on ships from Marseille. Then he began to do it for families he didn't know. And then, he said, he got caught.

He knocked back what was left of his marc and poured another.

"I don't like involvement. I don't like what I had to do during the war. I don't like choices, but in order to survive in some situations, you have to choose. And then you're stuck and you keep on doing what you know how to do."

That was, in effect, the end of le Baron's version of his personal story. All he told me was that later, after the war was over, he came out to Corsica to rest.

"I have to live with this past," he said. "We all do. It is like some chronic disease that flares up from time to time. And so I came out here with Isabelle, and we live in the country, in isolation, trying to stay healthy. I want nothing more to do with the world, you understand. I learned this from Isabelle."

He had married late in life, he said. He had met her at a friend's villa in Nice at a dinner party.

"She was the shy one you see at such events, bright-eyed and seemingly interested in the chatter, but also preoccupied and silent. Later we talked privately. She had all the usual traumas of war, don't you know. We all did, I suppose. But she was deter-mined to avoid any remembrance. She loved silence and flowers, and she was the opposite of most of the other women I had known. I found refuge in her silences. We married. And then I remembered Corsica. The peace of nature.

"And so I read. I clip hedges like a peasant, tend the roses. It is my pleasure. But on some nights I am restless, the old animal past rises up on its haunches. It is then that you see me at the café."

Marie and Isabelle came down the path from the house at this point, moving speedily, I thought, for such an unhurried entertaining evening.

Marie said bluntly that she was tired and had a headache, and that we really should be going. Le Baron glanced at Isabelle, I noticed, but otherwise seemed only slightly surprised, and so with much thanks and a few cool kisses, we were ushered out the wide front door to the car. We stood on the front steps for a few minutes, with a little more polite small talk, and then Marie and I crossed the gravel drive to the car. The two of them stood in the doorway, bathed in the light from a wrought-iron lamp beside the entrance, watching us go.

I steered the Citroën down the gravel drive and out onto the road back through the town.

Marie was uncharacteristically subdued during the drive, cool even, and when we got back to the café we sat in the car in the parking area and talked for a while. She was stiff and strangely formal.

"What did you think?" I asked.

"I think your friends are despicable people," she said finally. "I am sure of it. They are spies or criminals of some sort. All those silly rumors about contraband and forgery, they're not accurate. Those people are worse . . ."

"What are you talking about? Did Isabelle tell you something?"

"No. She said nothing. But they are loathsome people. Low-class scum of the earth. That's how I know. That Isabelle, she is unbalanced, the things she wanted me to do with her. You too. You and I together. And they would watch. It was despicable. Vile people. Pigs. I never want to see them again."

chapter fifteen Le Grand Bal

On one of my afternoons off a week later, I went up into the hills by myself to see if I could find old Fabrizio and have another chat.

I walked into town, passed through the back streets on foot, and began to hike up the road into the hills. The houses were fewer here, and after a ten- or twenty-minute walk, clear from side roads and other turnings, I began to hitchhike. A few cars, driven by older men with tinted eyeglasses, passed without stopping; a couple of fully loaded trucks lumbered on, and then the traffic, such as it was, died out for a while. I entertained myself by walking slowly upward, trying to identify the profusion of wildflowers that grew along the verges.

When I was well above the town, I came upon a few loose cows grazing by the side of the road. They looked up at me and watched closely as I passed, as if recognizing a foreigner in their midst.

Every time I would hear a car coming I would turn and hold out my thumb, and eventually a talkative man with a thick island accent took me upward for a few miles before he had to turn off. I walked on, rather enjoying myself, even if I wasn't able to find the turn for the track up to Fabrizio's compound.

At the village of Sant'Antonio, after a stiff climb to the center, I stopped and had a beer and asked if anyone there knew the old man. They had heard of him, but they laughed when I mentioned his name and twisted their fingers up alongside their temples — a screw loose, in so many words.

The views from Sant'Antonio were splendid. It was perched high on a steep crag, like an eagle's nest, and provided a nearly 360-degree vista of the whole region known as the Balagne, which included the towns of Ile Rousse and Calvi to the northwest. The little hill towns in this region were said to be among the most picturesque in Corsica; in fact Sant'Antonio itself was apparently the oldest continuously settled village on the island, having been established sometime in the ninth century and occupied in the time of the Pisan rule over the island.

The many little villages perched on their hilltops were in decline in those years, the younger people having left the island in search of work. But some of them had been repopulated by people from the continent seeking solace, or refuge, or — in one case — anonymity. Southwest of Sant'Antonio in the agricultural village of Calenzana, not far from Calvi, there were said to be a few high-level members of the French underworld living out their lives in relative isolation and peace.

In spite of the loss of the local population, however, there were still a few local crafts being carried out, and there was still a certain amount of subsistence agriculture — olive groves, cheese-making, a few vineyards, and of course, goats, cows, and feral pigs.

In Sant'Antonio I was told that Fabrizio — they thought — lived back in the direction I had come from. On the way up I had noticed what I thought was a familiar turn, but I had been too involved with the talking driver to ask him to stop. Now at a car park below the village, I hitched a ride north again, and got out at the turn.

Higher along the little spur road I saw the track to Fabrizio's and hiked up to the old man's compound.

He was there, but I had to reintroduce myself before he offered me his traditional glass of plonk. After a little small talk about Pierrot, I tried to ask him a few questions about le Baron again, but without the presence of Pierrot, he was far more polite and less talkative, and merely said yes or no to my reiteration of the various le Baron stories. It appeared that I was making him uncomfortable.

After another glass of wine, I told him I had had dinner at le Baron's house a few nights earlier.

"Big place," he said.

"Yes, very nice gardens."

"What did you eat?"

I described the dinner.

"And so you met his wife," he said.

I said that I had, and he merely nodded and grunted.

It was interesting that after our first meeting he was not as talkative as he had been. I began to wonder if perhaps he had gotten word somehow that I was checking his story. Certainly it was clear to me by this time that there were tales to be told here on this part of the island, and that everyone knew more or less what those stories were, but that there was no need to expand on them — especially not certain tales.

To change the subject, I began to talk about my work at the Rose Café and Vincenzo and Max, whom he said he knew, and also Jean-Pierre, whom he said he had heard of.

"Is he the one who is married to that artist woman they call Micheline?" he asked.

I told him he was, and he merely nodded and said no more, although he obviously knew more.

I had my notebook with me, and I had tucked a few wildflowers into the pages, so I took them out and asked if he knew what they were.

At this he became more animated. He knew each one, and he also knew their uses, and along with their names he offered a long string of remedies, flavorings, potions, and other folkloric qualities. Much of this was lost on me, even though he was speaking in French. But I did manage to note the names. (Not that that did any good either; I never could find the English equivalent for most of them.)

I was intrigued by a thyme-scented plant he called *sarriette*, which he said he would cook with his goat stews. He also named some of the plants I was already familiar with, such as pimpernel, goat's beard, and myrtle, a common pot herb in Corsica, for which he named a few uses other than culinary. I think he said, among other benefits, it was good for the prostate.

In this same vein he snatched up a ranunculus-like sprig of leaves that he called *cuglione di prete*, which, if I understood the local term from my knowledge of Italian, meant "priest's balls." He identified another flower called *puncicula*, which he said was good for your fingernails and your hair. And he also identified a plant he called *herbe des moines* — monk's plant — which he said could help men resist temptations of the flesh. Also snakebites.

Like most older country people, Fabrizio spoke with his hands and was not shy about demonstrating, bodily, the uses for certain herbs, so it was easier to understand some of his plant identifications than his abstracted gossip about le Baron and others.

At one point he asked to see my book, with its scrawled notes and sketches.

He looked them over, turning the pages with his stubby thumb and nodding. "*Momento*," he said, and went back into the cascading heap of stones he used as his retreat.

When he came back, he had the notebook created by the German soldier who used to come up to his compound to talk about nature. Fabrizio had apparently forgotten that he had showed this to me on an earlier visit.

I flipped through pages — sadly, I should say — and found there a couple of sketches of wildflowers I either knew or had collected. There was something poignant in the old yellowed pages and Hansi's spidery ink sketches, browned-out now with age. Inscribed there was some element of the absurdity of human conflict that contrasted with the endurance of nature.

Fabrizio explained again the story behind the notebook, leaving out the fact that Hansi had been killed by his compatriots, I noticed.

I handed the book back to him and he looked through it himself, reviewing it.

"He was my friend," he said reflectively. "German. But not a bad sort."

Given the rumors about the old man as a mazzero, his knowledge of local uses of herbs allowed me to swing the questions around and ask him about witches and signadore and local voceratrice, the women who sing poetic laments over the body of a vendetta victim.

He tried to explain. I think he said that up here in the villages, when he was younger, many of these old traditions endured, but since the war the old world was passing.

"How about mazzeri?" I asked finally. "Are there any mazzeri left up here?"

"Any what?" he asked.

"Mazzeri!" I said, emphasizing the Italianate pronunciation.

"Mazzeri?" he said with finality, raising his voice.

"*Si, mazzeri*, are there any around here?" I asked in Italian.

He spouted a very long animated sentence in dialect, not one word of which I was able to catch.

"I see," I said, to be polite.

There followed another explanation, even longer. He waved his hand up toward the villages higher up in the hills, and swept his palms together and poked his thumb backward over his shoulder — no more left, in other words. At one point, though, he also drew his finger across his throat, indicating a foretold death, maybe, or perhaps a vendetta. I began to wish I had Pierrot with me to translate.

Whatever his explanations, the fact that he himself was rumored to be a mazzero did not seem to affect his answers to my questions, at least not as far as I could read it. As Vincenzo had said, probably the stories about him were just gossip from the women who lived high in the stone villages, cloistered in their kitchens and narrow winding streets with nothing to get excited about but newly settled Sardinians and Arabs, and the life of local eccentrics. Micheline told me that some of those older women had never left their tiny towns.

On my way back down to the main road, I started to think about the German officer again and felt a wave of sympathy for the man, even though he had lived at a remove from my world and was a Nazi. He was probably just a shy student type who never fit in, even in his own community, a member of the international company of naturalists who seem to spring up in all industrialized cultures.

Later, farther down the track but in this same reflective mood, the logical answer to all this obfuscation of le Baron's story came to me.

It should have been obvious from the first day.

Why should an island people with their own culture, their own histories, their own demons, and perhaps most importantly, a nasty reputation on the continent, share anything with a fresh young American (via Paris, no less) who comes rooting around in their personal affairs to uncover events that are best left unexplained? It occurred to me that I could have learned a thing or two from Prosper Mérimée, who, it was said, had the ability to come into a strange country, pick up the language quickly, and gain trust with the people and record their folklore.

Had I known at the time, I could also perhaps have learned a lot more about the culture of the interior from the Englishwoman Dorothy Carrington, who was living down in Ajaccio at that time and was perhaps the best English-speaking authority on the old traditions of Corsica. She set down her observations in her 1971 book, *Corsica: Portrait of a Granite Island*. Unfortunately I didn't know she even existed until her book appeared.

Every year in September, the town would sponsor a big costume ball in honor of nothing in particular, as far as I could determine. We out at the Rose Café were invited, of course, as were our current guests, and as the weekend of the festival approached, people set to work making costumes.

Marie determined she would go as Medora, the Greek slave girl from the ballet *Le Corsaire*. Chrétien, who was fond of all things Spanish, intended to be a Sevillian caballero, and Vincenzo said he wanted to be a pirate.

Maggs, who was generally enthusiastic about local events, was less interested in costuming herself and sat around the terrace in the afternoons, drinking beer and walking out to the Ile de la Pietra all alone. I think there had been some manner of show-down with Peter. She was spending more time with him, and once or twice even went out spearfishing with him and spent the time swimming and sunbathing while he cast to and fro among the rocks below the surface, looking to kill fish. André was not coming out to the café as often, I noticed, and when he did he seemed to avoid Maggs.

We had a more or less normal Saturday at the restaurant, but we posted a notice that we would be serving only a light, early dinner that evening so that we could all take off for the big event.

The morning was clear, but in midafternoon ominous yellow clouds began breaking over the mountain peaks, and the wind picked up. The scirocco, the hot, sandy wind off the Sahara, was preparing to blow in.

After we cleaned up from the light dinner, we all assembled and walked into town as a group. Jean-Pierre and Micheline led the loosely formed procession of our staff and guests. Jean-Pierre came as himself — more or less — dressed in a clean, white high-button tunic and a toque. Micheline wore Turkish harem pants tied at the waist with a red sash and a multitude of colorful scarves wrapped around her head. Chrétien was walking with Karen in his Spanish costume, and Karen — somewhat daringly given the fact that she was to be mixing with Corsican males from the interior — came as a streetwalker, wearing a short red skirt, net stockings, and a low-cut blouse that revealed her ample bosom.

Marie had fashioned for herself a light-spangled bra and a gauzy, transparent green skirt that rode low on her hips and was held up by a flamboyant cloth belt, onto which she had sewn cheap baubles that she had purchased in town. She wore a silk-scarf headdress that was held in place with a twisted, brightly colored headband, and she had made up her face garishly with red rouge, lipstick, and an overload of mascara. In a burst of enthusiasm, she had painted a starburst of arrows above and below her eyes.

Marie had wanted me to go as a cowboy but although we tried, we could not find any cowboy boots, chaps, or ten-gallon hats. In the end I borrowed one of Pierrot's blue jumpsuits and an old paint-stained beret and came as a laborer. Hardly much of a disguise.

We also had with us, for safekeeping perhaps, Herr Komandante, who was dressed as a flaneur from the Riviera in white canvas trousers, a blue blazer, and a paisley cravat. I noticed also that he had rouged himself subtly, but he looked good that night, healthy from the sun, and well fed and recovered from his shame. Amusingly, Giancarlo, who was walking with Herr Komandante, had assumed a costume that divulged a certain amount of self-mockery. He came as the old pedant, il Dottore, from the commedia dell'arte.

In town, rather than weave through the streets, we followed the Promenade a Marinella along the harbor, and then turned up the Rue Louis Philippe to the Place Paoli, thus affecting a grander entrance to the square.

No one noticed.

There was a big stucco public building with green shutters at the eastern end of the central plaza where the dance was to be held. Posters had been plastered here and there around the cafés and public places, inviting all to attend, and officials had decorated the building with bunting, and the double doors were flung open and secured against the rising scirocco. Inside, in the warm light, we could see a riotous fling of color.

I thought I knew, from the wild Halloween parties I had attended back home, a little about costuming. But my experience paled in view of the scene in the hall before me. Here were the usual pirates in headscarves and earrings and eye patches, dressed in baggy red pantaloons and wide-sleeved shirts, some with big country daggers stuffed into their bright sashes. There were many harem girls with exposed midriffs and translucent skirts writhing to the music, and a woman attired as Mérimée's Colomba danced a wild jitterbug with a bandit d'honneur in his black corduroy and bright red cummerbund. Joan of Arc was there, dancing with a half-naked *peau rouge* — a red Indian. Madame du Barry was dancing with Louis XV, and many Hawaiian fire leapers in sarongs danced with hula-hula girls. The Queen of the Nile sailed through; several pharaohs paraded with Nubian slaves with golden armbands and charcoal-blackened faces, and all the characters from the commedia dell'arte were there too, dancing furiously — Columbine with Harlequin, Pantalone and Pierrette. The great braggart, Captain Scaramouch, frolicked in his seven-league boots, and big-bellied Punchinello with his huge crooked nose courted a fat maiden in a formal, bowing two-step. There were many monsters and devils and goat men of all types, and priests and nuns, cardinals — and even the Pope himself, a de Gaulle–like figure whom I had seen around the boule pitch from time to time. Here was a bright explosion of all the accumulated characters of European culture, all in motion and whooping and cutting up the floor to an American jazz number. It seemed to me that old Europe had collected here in some pantomime of history.

As soon as we entered, Marie grabbed my hand and dragged me out to the floor and began an energetic jitterbug, interspersed with sinuous turns and leaps and pirouettes, presumably imitating steps from *Le Corsaire*. I could hardly keep up with her, but she stayed with me, leading me around the floor, spinning off and ducking under my arm, freeing herself for a pas de chat or a jeté, and then returning to the pattern of ballroom steps. And when that number ended, finally, she fell into my arms, already in a sweat.

We went over to the back of the hall where there was a bar and picked up a beer, half of which she drained before I could get a sip.

"It's good here, no?" she said.

Thankfully, the band, which consisted of a piano, drums, a bass, an electric guitar, and a clarinet, started a slow French number, and Marie and I slid out onto the floor, the first ones out, and we twirled around, cheek to cheek, in a foxtrot. She was easy to dance with, so light on her feet I felt she was floating just above the floor. Periodically she fixed my eyes while we danced as if to say you are the only man in all the world, you exotic American cowboy.

We weren't alone for long, out on the floor. Harlequin danced by with Columbine, Madame du Barry swept past, a few pirates with slave girls or captured countesses tripped through. Chrétien danced cheek to cheek with the slatternly *poule*, the erstwhile contessa, much fallen from grace now. They were laughing together and throwing back their heads and gyrating to the music. I spotted Herr Komandante nearby, dancing in perfect form. He was with a heavyset woman about his age, who was dressed in a cheap evening gown and draped with costume jewelry. I noticed a line of uncostumed older men leaning against the east wall of the room, casting a cold eye on him. They needn't have worried. Herr Komandante loved women as well as boys, and danced all night with the older single ladies of the town, who were happy to glide around the floor in the arms of a powdered continental roué, no matter what his sexual persuasion.

The slow number segued into a jitterbug, and the crowd was off again. I tried to keep up with Marie, but she was tireless. So was everyone else. It was as if the hot wind of the scirocco had worked its way into the hall and was whipping up the dancers in spite of themselves. On and on it went in a hot caper, one jump after another, and whenever we took a break, or whenever there was a slower number, we could see the rough apache dancers, leaning together, arms clasped around one another's necks. Jacquis was here, in a striped jersey, dancing with a tight-skirted woman with spit curls. André went by, cheek to cheek with a drunken German woman in white sailor's trousers and a man's yachting cap pushed to the back of her head. Many other people from the yachts were there too, easily distinguished by their makeshift costumes — deck mops for hair, men dressed as women, a soldier with a ship's cooking pot for a helmet, women clothed in minimalist bikinis, heels, and pounds of jewelry. Even old Giancarlo was dancing. He had found a woman about his age — dressed in a 1920s sequined black gown and much rouged, as if for the stage — and they twirled around the floor during the slower numbers. I also saw tall Peter escorting Maggs in her schoolgirl outfit. Once I saw her look up at him and laugh, and later I saw her lay her head on his chest. They stuck together, drank too much, and tried to imitate the local dance style. I saw them kissing during one of the slow numbers, and at one point I saw Maggs purposely avoid eye contact with André, who was standing by the bar in the back of the hall, one foot propped back against the wall, squinting through his cigarette smoke.

And all the while out in the square, the scirocco was hammering at the shutters. One of the front doors broke free and slammed shut. When it flew open again, I saw a figure in white standing in the half-light of the plaza. Moving slowly, le Baron entered and slipped along a side wall, found a spot, and propped his foot back and lit a cigarette. He watched the dancers silently with a vacant, abstracted expression, smoking idly, his right arm supported at the elbow by his left hand.

Jean-Pierre and Micheline had been dancing off and on throughout the evening, sometimes disappearing out to the plaza to talk to friends, sometimes moving together in the slower numbers. Jean-Pierre was easy to spot in his tall white toque, as it floated through the turbans, Harlequin hats, and the great feathered Gainsboroughs and Mexican sombreros. At one point I saw le Baron catch Jean-Pierre's eye, and he and Micheline danced over and stopped to chat with him. They stood talking for a while and then shook hands, and he kissed Micheline on both cheeks and made to leave.

Just before he went out, he turned and looked back at the hall of revelers. The scirocco was whipping his hair forward, and he stood with his weight on his left leg, his right hand in his suit-coat pocket. For a minute he reminded me of a tired knight looking out over a field of battle where lately all human energies had been expended.

Then he turned and walked into the night, his white suit fading into the shadows.

It was the last time I saw him.

The evening rose and fell, the scirocco hammered at the shutters and then, uncharacteristically, weakened into a hot stillness. One by one the numbers slowed, and then finally the band announced the last dance.

Some people had already moved out to the plaza, and the remaining couples were blown across the floor like errant leaves swept by squalls and gusts. They clung together, their costumes askew, tired and half-drunk but reluctant to let the night go.

The music ended and the dancers sauntered offstage, arms draped around one another as the musicians packed their instruments.

When we came out to the plaza, it was strangely still without the surge of the scirocco. The cafés were emptying, the last of the coffees and aperitifs served, and the people were disappearing down back streets and along the promenade leading to the port where the dinghies for their yachts nosed each other at the quay.

Marie put her arm around my waist and leaned her head on my shoulder, and we went over to the promenade and walked away from the town. Farther along, the walk gave way to an unpaved track, and we followed this eastward toward the wilder shores on the opposite side of the harbor. There was a sandy spit below the track, and we crossed through the scrub and sat on the beach for a while, watching the lights wink out across the bay at the Rose Café and the great circle of constellations wheeling around the North Star.

Beyond the bay, I could see the shark-fin outline of the rocky coast and hear the lonely cries of night-flying shorebirds, the first of the southbound migrants, headed across the coasts for Africa.

"Are you going back to Paris after this?" Marie asked after a while. She sounded older somehow, more serious.

I told her yes, later, maybe sometime in early October, I would go back to school.

"Will you look me up? Will I see you again?"

"Sure," I said. "But this sounds like some kind of an ending. Are you leaving?"

"My parents. They are coming back. It won't be the same, and then when they leave, I have to go with them. It's so sad."

I didn't say anything for a minute. I was struck by an odd loneliness, a little frisson of fear. Whatever would I do now, in this remote, forbidding country, alone?

"I don't like it," I said.

She looked over and fixed my eyes. "Neither do I. I didn't expect this."

"I know what you mean," I said.

She kissed me suddenly and flung her arms around me and held on desperately and wouldn't let go. I grabbed her, and we rolled down together into the sand. I could smell her distinctive perfume mixed with salt and summer and the wild scent of the maquis.

The beach was still warm; the harbor was protected and calm; and the waters merely slapped at the shore. But out beyond the Ile de la Pietra, the hammer blows of the scirocco were still making themselves known, and the pitched waves were throwing themselves against the ancient Corsican granite again and again in a steady, rhythmic pulse, as if marking the passage of time.

In the end we stayed there all night.

M arie's parents showed up the following Thursday, as expected, and immediately wandered off to the village and the shops and bars with their restless Parisian energy. Marie withdrew and became bored and moody, and merely rolled her eyes heavenward whenever we were together with her parents, as if to say, have you ever met anyone as stupid as they are? Nevertheless, she was gracious about including me and admitting, in so many words, that this American cowboy was her *petit ami*, her current boyfriend.

One night, having made some arrangements with Jean-Pierre, they invited me to a dinner in town at a restaurant just off the plaza that specialized in island cuisine. Giancarlo came along, and they selected a table on the verandah from which we could look down across the square to the building where the dance had been held the weekend before. I couldn't help but think back on the bright revels of that evening and my night with Marie on the beach. She sat across from me and we exchanged glances from time to time, probably sharing the same memories.

Giancarlo and Marie's parents spent the evening analyzing the current political situation, with Franco and Salazar in control on the Iberian Peninsula, a right-wing coalition of generals and colonels waiting offstage down in Greece, and, more importantly as far as they were concerned, the OAS blowing up apartment buildings and gunning for de Gaulle and planning for some kind of new France, which would be very like the old France — only worse. Marie's parents feared a second wave of fascism, but

Giancarlo, who had the advantage of age, was arguing the bigger picture.

"My dear friends," he pronounced at one point. "Not to worry. It will all come to a sad and simpering end. I accept your point on the dangers of fascism, of course. But I must disagree with your concept of the communal state and the redistribution of property."

He sipped his wine, replaced the glass carefully on the table, touched the sides of his lips with his napkin, and announced that he would continue.

"In point one, I must argue that power by means of violence is a great disorder, but that that disorder begets an order of sorts. Id est, the streets are clean. The trains run on time. No crime in the streets. But you will of course agree that a perfect order is, enfin, disorder, and whether that order is sustained by monarchy, despot, or the Comintern makes no difference. I mean to say that the leader is dead in our time. There shall be no more Caesars. The Führer is dead by his own hand! Il Duce is hung upside down in a square by his people. All dead. And now Europe will give birth to a benign liberal democracy."

He paused again.

"You can see the modern-day progenitor of this new world aborning, there below us."

He waved his arm and spread his hand to the statue on the square.

"Behold! Pasquale Paoli, with his mad idea of a liberal constitutional government. And now, from the sperm of that first failed revolution, a new form of king shall be conceived and that king shall be named 'Charter.' And Charter, like Saturn, will consume all its children: the nations and the kingdoms and the empires and all the borders in between."

I looked down at the square with its statue of the Corsican liberator. But I could not help but also notice the two ice cream stands on the north side of the square, and near the statue, the blinking lights of the carousel circling round and round, carrying its passengers to the next generation.

I had had perhaps too much to drink that night, and for the first time, deigned to venture an opinion.

"The only emperor is the emperor of ice cream," I said.

They all turned on me with blank stares. Marie laughed and covered her mouth.

"What is that you say, my son?" Giancarlo asked.

"Sorry," I said. "It's just a quote from an American poet."

They all nodded politely and dashed headlong back into their various predictions.

The next day, a Friday, Giancarlo took a hired car down to Calvi and left on the afternoon ferry. On Sunday, Marie spent most of the morning packing her bags. I hadn't seen much of her over the weekend. It was the end of summer and turned out to be a busy period. I had a lot of fish to clean, and the tables were full throughout lunch and dinner. I was constantly at work. Whenever we managed to get a few minutes together, Marie seemed sad and pouting.

When the inevitable Sunday evening push rolled around, the workload was even worse, with whole battalions of soldierly dishes streaming in, and pots and pans piling in stacked mountains on the stone sink counters. It was a hot night, and I had to work furiously to keep up, my sleeves rolled high on my arms and the front of my apron soaked and stained with food.

Just before she and her parents carted their baggage down to the quay to board, Marie came into the scullery and, without saying anything, spun me around by my shoulders, threw her arms around me, and kissed me, pressing her body against my wet apron.

"Call me," she said.

"I will."

We finally managed to say goodbye to one another and she backed out the door looking sad, as if she was about to cry.

She pushed out her lower lip, looked at me from under her brows, and waved weakly with her fingers.

"Cowboy," she whispered.

Half an hour later, in a lull between courses, I stepped out of the scullery and climbed the little rise behind the back door. The white ferry was just making its way out of the dark harbor, and as I watched, it cleared the jetty and made its turn to the north, and then headed across the night waters to Nice.

Its lights were bright against the black sea, but slowly they grew smaller and smaller and finally disappeared, and after that there was nothing but the distant *thud* of the waves and the canopy of stars, the Great Bear circling above the Ile de la Pietra.

One by one, the players left the stage.

Herr Komandante packed his bags one day and left midweek in a hired car for Calvi. The four of us on the staff stood with him on the terrace to say goodbye.

He shook my hand warmly before he got in the car.

"Be brave in life," he said.

I was a little mystified and started to say something, but by that time he was in the backseat of the car, waving from the window and smiling and showing his teeth.

"I always liked him," Jean-Pierre said, as the car bumped down the causeway, "even if he was a German."

"He was a good German," Chrétien said.

"Not a bad sort," said Micheline.

The next weekend Maggs and Peter left. I saw their bags out on the terrace with Peter's diving gear and knew what was coming. Peter spotted me in the dining room and shook my hand formally, and later Maggs sought me out in the scullery and kissed me on both cheeks in the French style and held my wet hands in hers.

"You will come and see us now in London, when you have time."

I said I would.

"Take the night train from Paris. You can stay with us in Kensington. We have a room. We'll have a dinner party."

I said again that I would come. She was looking at me with that fixed stare. And then spontaneously, she embraced me in a motherly way, rubbing my back vigorously.

"Have a good season in Paris," she said. She kissed me again and walked out.

Chrétien asked to borrow Jean-Pierre's Citroën one day, explaining that he would like to drive Karen and her troupe over to Calvi to catch the midweek ferry. I was free that afternoon and went along with them. We all piled in: Laurent, Clotilde, and I in the backseat and Karen lolling against Chrétien's shoulder in the front.

It was a subdued drive. Everyone was sorry to be leaving, and since we had some time, we took a turn on a side road and drove down to a beach Chrétien knew about and sat by the water watching the waves.

Chrétien and Karen took a walk down the shore and disappeared behind some high rocks at the east end of the cove. They were gone for a while and looked disheveled and flushed when they came back. Just before we left, Karen waded out into the water and stood with her skirts hoisted and tucked into her waistband. She looked like a sea nymph, there with her white dress bunched like a tunic and the light waves breaking over her thighs. She stood alone for a long time, staring out to sea, then she turned and came striding back through the waters. I think she had been weeping.

"Let's go," she said. "Let's just get it over with."

In Calvi, we sat in a quayside café waiting for the ferry, which after half an hour or so appeared in the harbor. A band had assembled to greet a visiting dignitary from France, and the players stood around in a loose group, smoking and talking. They wore a strange collection of hats and uniforms from various wars and government agencies — army, navy, police, and fire — and they had old battered coronets and drums. The gangplank was lowered, and when the dignitary came out from the passageway the band struck up an off-key version of the "Marseillaise," and the petty official descended. He had lost an arm and had tucked his coat sleeve into the left pocket of his gray suit, and he waved with his right hand as he picked his way down. No one seemed to notice his grand arrival except for a few men, also in suits, who stood on the quay to meet him.

Finally, it was time to board. Karen and Chrétien stood

nuzzling at the gangplank, promising to find one another. I kissed Clotilde and shook hands with Laurent, and they all walked slowly up the gangplank — Karen in her white shift, her small backpack slung over her shoulder, and her mass of hair flying in the sea wind. On the little staging area at the top, she turned and waved.

"What a beauty," Chrétien said sadly. "What a wild white horse. Captured in the marshes of the Camargue. Never tamed."

Ile Rousse grew dull after that.

I shared coffee and hot baguettes with Pierrot each morning as usual, but except for the adventure of the big dance, there didn't seem to be much to talk about. I went for my daily swim, cleaned the dishes, cut fish, and worked the dinner shifts, and when I was free, wandered into the square to watch the boules players. The same troupe was there, of course. They were there before I came. They would be there long after I left.

On some afternoons I continued on from the square through the village and up into the hills, and followed sheep trails to nowhere. Birds were everywhere in the maquis — warblers and finches, thrushes and bee-eaters, all southbound. One afternoon there I met a cross-eyed goatherd who told me winter would be coming soon up in the mountains. Another day I went out to the Ile de la Pietra and circled under the Genoese tower and made my way along the shore, clambering over the rocks, resting from time to time to watch the sea and the sky beyond. But it was lonely there in the coves, empty, with only the pointless rise and fall of the green waves, the echoes of past conversations, and only the cormorants and the alien limpets, periwinkles, and snails as company.

With no woman to occupy him Chrétien grew more talkative. He sat with me after dinner, spilling out his plans to flee to Andalusia in the spring with Karen, where he said they would go to the big horse fair in Seville and then to the feria.

"We will drink sherry under the walls of the alcazar," he said. "And she will dance with the gypsies of the Macarena. During Holy Week we will make love in an upstairs pension above the Serpiente as the Christian processions pass below us in the streets."

"Sounds good," I said.

I meant it. I knew at some point I would have to leave Corsica and my suspended life at the Rose Café, but I was not looking forward to Paris and its seamless gray skies. I knew also that I would at some point have to deal with the little problem of the American draft board. But I was ready for some new direction, something other than the nightly round of cafés and bars and futile political chatter. In fact, as things turned out, I finally began to write. A year later I went back to college in America, managed to avoid the draft and the war, and after a little more wandering, began freelancing.

Sometimes in September, new guests would arrive, but they were older people mostly — a few English pensioners, an older German couple who would come down for breakfast in their slippers and bathrobes. There was a strange Belgian man with a younger woman, who seemed more like his secretary than his girlfriend, and also a very polite but very boring couple from Brittany who had never traveled outside of France and, like the nineteenth-century English travelers before them, thought Corsica was an exotic foreign country.

One night I heard a wind come up. The noise woke me, as usual, but I noticed that there was something different in the sound and went outside. There was a new scent in the air, a sharper, saltier smell. The mistral was beginning to blow, the cold north wind that sweeps down off the Rhône Valley in France.

The next day was bright and clear, and the wind was charging down across the harbor, stretching the flags out straight and slapping the halyards of the few yachts that were left on their moorings. By late afternoon it set the whitecaps flying, and it blew all the following night, howling over the Ile de la Pietra, forecasting winter and discontent.

That evening, Jean-Pierre turned the kitchen over to Vincenzo and went off with Micheline in the car without telling anyone where they were going. I was mystified by this, since they usually shared their plans with the staff. I asked Vincenzo if he knew where they had gone and he dodged the question, which of course only served to whet my curiosity. Finally, to shut me up, he told me that they had gone out to le Baron's place.

"Just a little business affair. Then a little dinner," he said.

"On business?" I asked. "They have a business together?"

"I don't know," he said. "Maybe. Something like that."

I let it go. I was finally getting used to mysteries.

A few nights later, after dinner, Jean-Pierre poured me a glass and sat with me out on the terrace.

"It looks like the season is over," he said. "It is finished. And so for you . . ." He spread his palms with a helpless shrug.

"I know," I said. "I have to get back anyway."

"The *Bagheera* is coming in a couple of days; I can arrange passage for you to Marseille," he said.

We drank quietly, watching the harbor and the causeway,

as one by one the cardplayers began to arrive: Max first, then Jacquis, then André. They greeted us, shaking hands all around, lazily, and went over to their table on the harbor side of the terrace and sat staring out at the harbor. Waiting. After a while, Jean-Pierre said he should probably join them. He rose, walked over and sat down, and accepted whatever hand was dealt to him.

I left with Chrétien a few days later. We stood on the quay with Vincenzo, Jean-Pierre, and Micheline, smoking and making small talk and watching the stevedores argue over the great nets of cargo that were lowered from the decks.

Jean-Pierre drew me aside to say goodbye and pressed a thick manila envelope into my hands.

"For you," he said. "For all the fish and dishes."

We shook hands all around and kissed and pounded one another's shoulders, and Lucretia buried me in her arms and sniffled. Then Chrétien and I boarded and stood in the stern as the old vessel rumbled and growled, made its turn, and headed out from Ile Rousse harbor.

The freighter rounded the jetty and laid a straight course northward, a few gulls following and a long stream of dancing furrows spreading astern in a north-facing arrow. The promenade along the shore grew smaller; the red-tiled roofs of the Rose Café receded, blended with the surrounding rocks, and then disappeared. Then the town diminished, leaving only the judgmental nuns hovering above. Then the nuns faded, and all I could see were the jagged, indifferent heights of the interior.

For a while, the island floated above the horizon, a gray wash of abstracted peaks, unattached to anything tangible in the midst of a turquoise sea. The engines thrummed below me with a rhythmic *thud*. I caught a whiff of the maquis, and as I watched, the ambiguous peaks slowly faded to memory — a rose-red island where blue-green valleys swept down to the sea, and sea rolled out to the wide azure sky.

Epilogue

In a quiet moment on the deck, while Chrétien was asleep, I opened the envelope and found there six crisp $20 American bills. I had not seen American notes in a long time, and they had a clean sharpness to them that I had forgotten. I hid them in my pack and spent the rest of the journey sleeping and daydreaming of Paris and Marie and the lonely, cross-eyed goatherd I had met coming down from the mountains. It struck me that I never did get a chance to say goodbye to old Fabrizio, although I had told Pierrot to tell him I was leaving. It also occurred to me that I never said goodbye to le Baron either, whoever he was.

Although I learned more details than I sometimes cared to hear about the sad pasts of the visitors at the Rose Café, I never did learn very much about the private lives of the regulars who frequented the place. And mainly, I never did learn anything definitive about le Baron.

In spite of my dogged snooping, I never came to know which of the intertwined stories about his past was true. Was he the generous benefactor who aided the local people? Was he the miserable dealer in Jewish properties, as Fabrizio had told me? Was he an important player in the French resistance? Was he the capu of a successfully obscured smuggling ring? Or was he a skilled forger of exit visas and a financier who liberated desperate Jewish families, as he himself explained? Or was le Baron perhaps a little of all of that and then some?

In spite of the odd ending to the little dinner party with Marie, because of the apparent sincerity of his story and the epic sadness and penumbral tones of his delivery, I had more or less come to accept his own version of his tale — even if it wasn't true. But the fact is, in the end, I didn't really care.

It was from the hunt for le Baron that I first came to learn the value of narrative — the rich fabric of truth, supposed facts, misinterpretation, delusions, myths, legends, and inventions that makes up the history of a place — or a person. I learned that perhaps it didn't matter which tale was authentic.

Chrétien and I spent a hideous night in the Marseille train station, trying to sleep on the hard benches amid the drunks and clochards and petty criminals who had taken shelter there. We caught the morning train the next day and slept most of the way up to Paris, and I went back to my old haunts on the Left Bank.

A few days after I settled in, I took one of the $20 notes to the Bank of France to get it changed. The teller, a mousy woman with tinted glasses and a brown suit, took the bill, snapped it flat, and inspected it.

"One moment please," she said and went off to a back room.

She was gone for a long time.

I waited, tapping my fingers on the counter, and after a while a heavyset, smooth-skinned man came over and angrily pushed the bill through the window.

"This is counterfeit," he said.